INCENDIARY ART

INCENDIARY ART

POEMS

PATRICIA SMITH

TRIQUARTERLY BOOKS / NORTHWESTERN UNIVERSITY PRESS

EVANSTON, ILLINOIS

TriQuarterly Books
Northwestern University Press
www.nupress.northwestern.edu

Copyright © 2017 by Patricia Smith. Published 2017 by TriQuarterly Books / Northwestern University Press. All rights reserved.

Printed in the United States of America

10   9   8   7   6   5   4   3   2   1

Library of Congress Cataloging-in-Publication Data

Names: Smith, Patricia, 1955– author.
Title: Incendiary art : poems / Patricia Smith.
Description: Evanston, Illinois : TriQuarterly Books/Northwestern University Press, 2017.
Identifiers: LCCN 2016036601 | ISBN 9780810134331 (pbk. : alk. paper) |
    ISBN 9780810134348 (e-book)
Subjects: LCSH: Till, Emmett, 1941–1955—Poetry. | African Americans—Poetry.
Classification: LCC PS3569.M537839 I53 2017 | DDC 811.54—dc23
LC record available at https://lccn.loc.gov/2016036601

The paper used in this publication meets the minimum requirements of the American National Standard for Information Sciences—Permanence of Paper for Printed Library Materials, ANSI Z39.48–1992.

Contents

I. Incendiary

INCENDIARY ART

I
INCENDIARY

That Chile Emmett in That Casket

Photo, Jet *magazine, Sept. 15, 1955*

Sometimes the page was tacked, flush against plaster with a pearl hatpin,
or jammed into a dime-store frame with a glowing Jesus. In some kingly

front rooms, its place was in the shadowbox, propped on one ripped edge,
or laid curly-cornered on the coffee table, smudged and eaten sheer

with the pass-around. In the kitchen, it was blurred by stew smoke
or pot liquor–blotched until somebody got smart enough to scotch-tape

it to door of the humming fridge, and the boy without eyes kept staring.
Mamas did the slow fold before wedging it into their flowered plastic

coin purses, daddies found a sacred place in pleather wallets right next
to the thought of cash. And at least once every week, usually on Sunday

after church or when you dared think you didn't have to speak proper
to that old white lady who answered the phone at your daddy's job,

or when, as Mama said, you *showed your ass* by sassin' or backtalking,
the page would be pulled down, pulled out, unfolded, smoothed flat,

and you had to look. *Look, boy.* And they made sure you kept looking
while your daddy shook his head, mumbling *This why you got to act*

right 'round white folk, then dropped his smoke-threaded gaze to whisper
Lord, they kilt that chile more than one time. Mama held on to your eyes—

See what happen when you don't be careful? She meant white men could
turn you into a stupid reason for a suit, that your last face would be silt,

stunned in its skid and worshipped, your right eye reborn in the cave
of your mouth. *Look!* she screeched. You did. But then you remembered

there weren't any pictures of *you* in the house, pinned high on the wall,
folded up tight up against the Lord, toted like talisman in wallet or purse.

You'd searched, woe climbing like river in your chest. But there were
no pictures of you anywhere. You sparked no moral. You were alive.

Enigma of the Shadowbox Swine

What was the import of the wee porcelain piglet?
Nobody really knew. But there it blared, zippy-eyed,
nuclear, curly tail ass-backed by a reflection of itself.
On a prime shelf, often joined by its more mystical

kin—unicorns, roosters with lips, tawdry dragons
gazing deep into days they didn't have—the moppet
bore no resemblance whatsoever to the fragrant
carcass we siphoned of blood and scraped clear

of bowels for the reunion barbecue. Every Negro
household had at least one shatter-prone piglet
as treasured keepsake, swiped lovingly with Pledge
every other Sunday, shuffled fro and to depending

on the angle of morning light. As decreed, the Lord
was represented, wistful on the sweat-stained back
of an old AME fan, or ceramic and indigo-eyed,
all-knowing, always crucified. And there was that

funeral program for Uncle Walter, Mama's big brother
who got old and older then just wasn't anywhere, but
sure did *look like he could just sit on up outta that
casket,* and a nicked souvenir saucer from Natchez,

with a dewy cotton field undulating in pastel steam.
Higher up, that grease-fingered still of dead dead
Emmett as deterrent, next to a tiny gold-rimmed
teacup—all we knew of elegance—and that one

murky Polaroid of gray, unreachable relatives.
But always, stark center, our plump-cheeked porker,
a gilded city hog crafted to remind us of where we
had come from, what we had come to live high on.

Incendiary Art

The city's streets are densely shelved with rows
of salt and packaged hair. Intent on air,
the funk of crave and function comes to blows

with any smell that isn't oil—the blare
of storefront chicken settles on the skin
and mango spritzing drips from razored hair.

The corner chefs cube pork, decide again
on cayenne, fry in grease that's glopped with dust.
The sizzle of the feast adds to the din

of children strutting slant, their wanderlust
and cussing, plus the loud and tactless hiss
of dogged hustlers bellowing past gusts

of peppered breeze, that fatty, fragrant bliss
in skillets. All our rampant hunger tricks
us into thinking we can dare dismiss

the thing men do to boulevards, the wicks
their bodies be. A city, strapped for art,
delights in torching them—at first for kicks,

to waltz to whirling sparks, but soon those hearts
thud thinner, whittled by the chomp of heat.
Outlined in chalk, men blacken, curl apart.

Their blindly rising fume is bittersweet,
although reversals in the air could fool
us into thinking they weren't meant as meat.

Our sons don't burn their cities as a rule,
born, as they are, up to their necks in fuel.

BlessBlessed

The burglar-barred church is warp, cardboard tilt. Spiced
smoke from salvation candles fogs the way in. Amen to
the lil' flailers, stiff in pinafore and patent, scalps greased
to glow, their squirming buoyed by the adamant yowling
of that organ and best-sit-still glower from the elders—those
dry baffling women who bop synthetic cinnamon heads,
their tinny voices straining for the rafters. Pious knots, frayed
but holding, they will be lovingly unraveled by Jesus soon
enough. In spit-shined halls doused in brocade, they pray
past Him in stunning rote, vowing to be undone by His
wounds, His azure-eyed swoop, some stuff He said, all
those hazy guide marks floundering in a confounding text.

This Sunday here, a real good Sunday. The reverend leaps,
threatening his natural spine, screeches of joy in the next
world: *Just no feeling like when the Lord brings you home
then wraps His arms around you.* Pews of the grizzled tingle.
Tambourines crash, ripple straight through to the backside,
Tony the organist stomps feral in his own sky, the choir sets
its sights on all those old bones. The Ghost shoves the agile
into the aisle. Stockings rip, matrons swirl, even the elders
careen in their seats when the reverend turns his lesson to fist:
*You might not wake up tomorrow. You might not make it
home tonight. But think hard on what glory you got waitin'!*
Service ends, or tries to, with a keen blaze lapping the walls.

From the basement wafts the siren stench of church supper—
chicken necks wilting in oil, collard greens, pork chops,
roasted yams rolled in brown sugar. Old folk groan gratitude,
say grace twice, slurp bounty from slow fingers, hiss *hush*
at those black obnoxious children. When they finally stand,

it is clearly an unfolding, pleats released and tumbling low
to brush brogans. Goodbye is *blessbless* and then the plod
from their church home to their own, passing corner stores
dank behind padlock and link, brick scarred with names
of ruined children. No matter which way they trundle, it's
a wade through a dimming drum. Cars buzz their skin, street
signs blur. They think it's faith poking them forward through
ambling turn and turn, but it's that devil, besotted by sermon,
who guides them home. Tonight, again, he'll sit patiently by
their beds, clucking suggestively in the direction of their rest.

Incendiary Art: MOVE, Philadelphia, 1985

It made sense to let the holocaust flaunt its swallow.
Only Africa noticed. The bomb spit-rained revelation
and vanishing, it rained skin and windows. On every
head, every wall. Headlines sang of complicated hair,
referred to water pooled just beneath the fold, out
of the way of burn, just out of the way of government.
Veering as bluing lesson through veins of boulevard,
a strident heat eclipsed the struggling breath. The stink
of shifted skin, monstering the air, held on, held on,
steel-jawed, strangler. Obsessed with order, bullhorns
blared nouns that unreeled vaguely like continents
while manned squad cars spun in their own sweat.

Spying on smothered drums and death throes, 6 pm
maestros rattled urgent update, used their perfectly
flat mouths to romance *cult* and *threat,* hiss *resist,*
debate the absence of cry and cringe. They passed
verdict while babies twirled and leapt in the wildfire's
lemony core and cinders snapped in perplexing braid.
No utter tenet whispered forecast of the scattering
regiment, stench of shea, the gorgeous collapsing
choreography of a vexed and bumbling infantry,
vendetta as dread. One little soldier was torched back
to birth. His ash eddied, drifted past domes of rule,
settled. In the swelling pile of him, rumor glittered.

Emmett Till: Choose Your Own Adventure

Mamie Till had hoped to take her son Emmett on a vacation to visit relatives in Nebraska. Instead, he begged her to let him visit his cousins in Mississippi.

Turn to page 14 if Emmett travels to Nebraska instead of Mississippi.

Incessantly, his mother quotes her God
while wrestling with the Plymouth's snarl and clunk.
The country's hellish breadth, its dank facade
conspire to make him blue and snappish, drunk
with dozing. Windows blur with foliage
and sweep. At roadside stops, the poison-eyed
and devilish slurp their tepid Cokes and gauge
his spine. Pretending he's preoccupied
with being from a place they can't decode
and knowing what they don't, he steels his back
against their hawk and spittle 'til the road
and Mamie call. To swagger past the pack,
he's learned to turn their threats to anecdote
and chuckle at the squeeze that begs for throat.

The Then Where

It's not supposed to happen here . . .

—Caitlin Viccari, a resident of Newtown, Connecticut, after 26
    children died in the shooting at Sandy Hook Elementary School,
    New York Daily News

In most of *here,* with its constant fields of stomped sienna, nothing much happens
beyond riotous yawn, ill-judged trajectory. Signs, nailed to torsos, point the way
to record-shattering skillets and gargantuan balls of twine, always elsewhere,
far down unbraided interstates, silent except for semis slicing through.
The desperate stuttering neon of commerce peppers the highway's fringe, preys
on the gluttonous minivan. We are the fretful hue of a shriveling copper wind,

all wobbling toward a noble, sunstruck end, witnesses to the patient unwinding
of a country where the sound of weeping is a prelude to sleep. And what happens?
Bawling willows, paperbark maples with storm-scarred limbs, men who praise
the sleek symmetry of smoke. Often we awake to violent daybreaks weighed
down with gilt. Toothy, malicious cities maneuver our necks to lead us through
alleyways, down chattering boulevards, into the maws of splintered doors where

the notion of *here* is hastily clawed against a flattened backdrop, into places where
the doubly negated screech double negatives and beg for the brief respite of a wind
against their skin. Staking teary claim to *Oh say can we see,* slapdashing through
lyric and mutilating that meandering key, we still want a verse that just happens
not to be there, one enamored of boys and their wormy canines, boys living way
beyond the mint religion of trees, sun-slapped boys, legs like carbines, who pray

east toward their sun, the blue-blinged pulse of firepower. Where's *their* praise,
that slant-rhymed yelp from shining sea to sitting sewage, reaching places where
tots slurp warm dairy, dress oddly and toddle into the barrels of guns? Once, way
past my birthright, craving *here,* I crossed the united heart in a car with the wind

at its ass, I crooned a twangy ballad that explains how restless sojourns happen,
how an unsettle in the paunch can lay open a road. So many *theres* tingle through

so many trigger fingers. My itchy digit obsesses on that road there, straight through
the scabbed gaze of the Natchez pump jockey, *nigra* a syrup on his tongue. Praise
him and the county roads, hammered with flags and directive, that led to him, hapless
two-lanes slicing through the bodies of children, past itty paint-perked tombs where
the dead lust continually for breath and mileage. We need a song that cages the wind
and keeps it at our backs, steering, shoving us through blurring vistas until one way

is *here.* Here. Egged on by gasoline's creamy reek and billboards of mouths, away
from fat bank accounts and the ragged rims of community, we blaze giddily through
Moline, Camden, Philly, Saugerties, we flee *there* while some clunky clock winds
down. Wowed by caffeine and donuts dipped in snow, we hum stanzas praising,
hailing the whole sweet muddled everywhere of it. The calendar flips, here where
murder strums its bloated belly, picks its teeth with the edges of maps. And happens.

Incendiary Art: Chicago, 1968

Nobody expected Goldblatt's to burn so fast.
Heard it said the store was flat before Martin's
blood was cold. A slapping stink turned the air
toxic—Dacron, plastic necklaces and earbobs,
rose-dotted acrylic Easter cardigans, reams
of forged patent leather, mirrored shadowboxes,
hundreds upon hundreds of knockoff Barbies
(flinty breasts still perked past combustion),
shiny cardboard living room suites sloshed
in wood hues, stacked cartons crammed with
eerily patient layaway tickets. Who knew our
pudgy American dream was so combustible?
Anyone could read the mind of the young boy
careening down Madison Street, rabidly clutching
a coveted pair of what he was convinced were
Converse All-Stars, the sneaks clearly on fire:
*Run some hot water in the sink, put a little Tide
on a rag, wipe all the burnt off, these gon' be
alright.* They sizzled in the moonwash, mad-ass
light lapping at the laces. When they cooled off,
one shoe showed blue, the other red. And *shit,*
they were different sizes. Cramming in his toes,
he wore them anyway, stumbling into daytime
trailing tendrils of smoke. Spouting triumph
amid the reeking ruins, he limped with conjured
pride, careful to hide his raw and swollen hands.

Reemergence of the Noose

Some lamp sputters
its dusty light
across some desk.
Some hand, shaking,
works the strained
rope, twisting and knifing,
weaving, tugging tight
a bellowing circle. Randy
Travis, steamy drawl
and hiccup on the staticky
AM, backs the ritual
of drooping loop.
Sweat drips an awful
hallelujah. God glares
askance, but the artist
doesn't waver—wrists
click cadence, knots
become a path to what
makes saviors. The sagging
hoop bemoans a need
to squeeze, its craving
for a breath within the ring.

Emmett Till: Choose Your Own Adventure

Fourteen-year-old Emmett Till was murdered after allegedly whistling at a white woman, Carolyn Bryant, the proprietor of a small store in Money, Mississippi. She also claimed that he showed her a picture of a white girlfriend he had back in his hometown of Chicago. The photo, which Emmett's mother insists came with the wallet, was said to have been of movie star Hedy Lamarr.

Turn to page 19 if Hedy Lamarr was actually Emmett's girlfriend.

His paltry age was never my concern—
I wrapped my pouting smoke around his heft
and crushed. The aim of our illicit burn
was sin, my purpose was the blatant theft
of everything that rendered him a child.
In shadowed rooms, my famous tongue was all
the blessing he could stand. I drove him wild,
I sucked him dry, my pudgy butterball.
Beneath my writhing sway, his color drained
and dripped its lazy drip onto the floor
'til every surface of our tryst was stained.
I waved his boyish body to the door.
His mama simply *had* to send him south—
my rampant crime, my little blabbermouth.

ReBirthday

On this slab of chilly steel, I am the morning's work,
your project after coffee and—yes, that woman's son.
Whistling to break the still in the room, you hold most
of my head in your hands. Your fingers gently adjust
an ear, probe a hollowed eye socket, flick chips of dried
blood away from a blown-open hairline. No one but you
and I hear as you inhale and, without exhaling, argue
clumsily with the four tangled downbeats of my name.

Grimacing, slow-edging away from the overwhelm,
you clutch the photo, glancing from swaggering smirk
to exploded child. The only sound is the blade's dull
skim as you free fluid from my blue mouth to whittle
a twisted smile. Reaching deep into your bag of tricks,
you pull out a nose, a sliver of chin, a jagged scalp,
and see them as just that—shards of skin, that scalp.
You've stitched my leaked light into the cave of your

own chest. That brown woman, gnarled with loss,
gestured wildly for you to rescript my days, wailing
that the bullets should have passed east of my name,
screeching *Please make him the way he was, as close
as you can to not dead, not dead, not gone,* and you

said *Yes.* You promised she'd be able to gaze at me
and whisper, with lunatic hope, *He looks just like he's
sleeping.* She's the reason you etch, snip and paste

with such stark focus, why you snap bones only to reset
them. I know you love this blanched landscape, fevered
fuse and stitch, patient attempts at ordinary hue, why

you've been so frantic with my breath. Whistling perk
past numb ritual, you stop now and again to behold
your gift to the woman who told you my name, just before
she showed you that dimming snapshot and begged you
Please, as best you can, my baby—

Incendiary Art: Birmingham, 1963

For Avery R. Young

Baby girls boom. Baby girls blow
and burn, skin balloons, booms.
Baby girls burn, boom. The Lord
dangles, festive and helpless.
Hymnals blacken while brown
baby girls pucker, leak. Blood jells,
muddles pigtail, makes lace stiff.
Baby girls blacken, crackle
in the vague direction of His hands
nailed still. Baby brown girl bodies
gap wide, wider, char and shut.

Runaway

First, somebody's got to run. There's no sport
in it otherwise. Everybody needs to be drunk
on sun first, then just straight drunk, and there

will be rot-tooth cackling, dog-tired horses
spewing snot, straps slashing gashes in dead
air. But somebody has to run like he wanna be

in a place he can't see, like Jesus blew a whistle.
The hunt needs a man who finally believes
the murmured come-ons of that blaring star,

who lingers a second too long in the red twist
of a preacher's promise, and thinks that being
free just may be that muted flash at the end

of his pointed finger. *Over there, out there,*
over yonder, north, always north, he chants,
his whole body primed, egged on by a fleeting,

luminous orchestra. But first he's got to run.
Everything he utters drips with a muddled,
sugary faith, his first halting steps click into

rhythm, and night lunges forward to scar him.
Sometimes he is minutes gone, maybe hours,
sometimes a day, before he realizes that all

land is throat, that it swallows and swallows
then dribbles a dust that lies and calls itself
light. The fear that he's on a journey that has

already ended sparks the smell, the salt that
just barely blues his skin. And the dog doesn't
know why or what it hates, it just knows that

Negro blur and the damn repeated spin of it.
The hound's strained heart is everything, an old
gray muscle gasping backbeat for a flailing rage.

Fevering against the leash, it snorts the deep
sweaty bowl of the runner's hat, one thinned
gray sock, an old work shirt. The cur quivers

with what it was born to do. There's just no
sport in it otherwise. Straining forward on their
steeds, the hunters whoop, addicts for the chase,

while that wily northern star spits its sickly light
along the length of the quest, nudging the huntsmen
and their quarry to very different versions of free.

10-Year-Old Shot Three Times, but She's Fine

Dumbfounded in hospital whites, you are picture-book
itty-bit, floundering in bleach and steel. Braids untwirl
and corkscrew, you squirm, the crater in your shoulder
spews a soft voltage. On a TV screwed into the wall
above your head, neon rollicks. A wide-eyed train
engine perfectly smokes, warbles a song about *forward.*

Who shot you, baby?
I don't know. I was playing.
You didn't see anyone?
I was playing with my friend Sharon.
I was on the swing,
and she was—
Are you sure you didn't—
No, I ain't seen nobody but Sharon. I heard
people yelling though, and—

Each bullet repainted you against the brick, kicked
you a little sideways, made you need air differently.
You leaked something that still goldens the boulevard.
I ain't seen nobody, I told you.
And at A. Lincoln Elementary on Washington Street,
or Jefferson Elementary on Madison Street, or Adams
Elementary just off the Eisenhower Expressway,
we gather the ingredients, if not the desire, for pathos:

an imploded homeroom, your empty seat pulsating
with drooped celebrity, the sometime counselor
underpaid and elsewhere, a harried teacher struggling
toward your full name. Anyway your grades weren't
all that good. No need to coo or encircle anything,

no call for anyone to pull their official white fingers
through your raveled hair, no reason to introduce
the wild notion of loving you loud and regardless.

Oh, and they've finally located your mama, who
will soon burst in with her cut-rate cure of stammering
Jesus' name. Beneath the bandages, your chest crawls
shut. Perky ol' Thomas winks a bold-faced lie from
his clacking track, and your heart monitor hums
a wry tune no one will admit they've already heard.

Elsewhere, 23 seconds rumble again and again through
Sharon's body. *Boom, boom,* she says to no one.

Emmett Till: Choose Your Own Adventure

Mamie Till insisted on an open casket so that the world could see
her son's mutilated body. More than 50,000 people filed past
during his funeral. Many screamed or fainted.

Turn to page 27 if Emmett's casket was closed instead.

We're curious, but his imploded eye,
the bullet's only door, would be the thing
we wouldn't want to see. We justify
his childish glint, and sigh, imagining
the knotted tie, the scissored naps, those cheeks
in rakish bloom, perhaps a scrape or two
beneath his laundered shirt. The mourners' shrieks
are tangled with an organ's point of view,
and someone moans Mahalia. Mamie's fanned
and comforted, her gorgeous fallen son
a horrid hidden rot. Her tiny hand
starts crushing roses—one by one by one
she wrecks the casket's spray. It's how she mourns—
a mother, still, despite the roar of thorns.

Hey, who you got in here?

My boy. Who you come to see?

My son. How old your boy?

21. How old your son?

19.

I seen you here a lot. Where you live?

West Side, over by Garfield Park. Where you live?

New York. Well, close to New York anyway.

And you come all this way?

Sho' don't feel like it.

Hot in here, ain't it?

Yep. Hot in here. Always is.

Wonder if the folks locked up is this hot all the time.

Hell, they in jail. Ain't sposed to be comfortable.

Hard coming out here.

Yeah. Hard.

I like your hair. Been thinking about getting those braids.

Take a long time.

I know. Three hours?

Girl, more than that. Your boy done cut all his hair off yet?

Uh-huh. Bald as the day he hit this world.

First thing they do, shave that head. Wonder why.

Ain't much else to do, I guess.

I guess.

They need to get some air in here. What they mad at *us* for?

Chile, you right. We ain't done nothing.

Always so damn hot.

Why your boy here? What he do? You don't have to—

Chile, I don't care. He in here for being stupid. Lord knows I—

Tried, I know.

Maybe he learn something in here. I tried to warn his black ass.
But they don't listen. Think they grown 'fore they grown.
I hear that. Shame to see so many of them in here though.
I know. Feel like we in another country.
I get tired of coming out here.
Me too.
Don't nothing change. Always so hot.
Girl, turn around, lemme see. I sho' like those braids. Real nice in back.
Thanks.
I need to get rid of this perm. Hell, gon' sweat it out in here.
Gotta remember to ask that boy if it's this hot—
Um-uh, all the time.
How long he gon' be in here?
End of next year. But he got another think coming if he think he—
Trying to come lay up in your house, huh?
Oh, he *think* he is. How long your chile here?
Another two years.
That's a long time.
Pass fast when you get old as me.
What you, 35? 36?
Almost.
Chile, I'm 40. Too old for this shit.
I can't get over how hot it is.
I'm gon' say something.
Me too, let's say something.
It ain't like *we* in jail.
Look. Look over there. You know that sister? She here a lot.
Uh-huh. Hey.
Hey.
Hey. How you doing? Figured we might as well speak.
We see you here a lot. Who you come to see?
My son. Who y'all come to see?
We got boys in here too. How old your boy?
He 20.

Damn, it's hot in here.
Girl, we was just saying.
We gon' say something about it this time. Don't make no damn sense.
Yeah, we gon' say something.
It's like they tryin' to—
Chile, I know. Kill us in here.

Incendiary Art: Los Angeles, 1992

Heard on the day they found Rodney King face down at the
bottom of a swimming pool: *Nigger could take an ass whuppin',*
but he couldn't swim! Ain't that something?

1

You can name yourself a man, walk taut and tall and will your voice
to stomp, but still be upended by demons, ain't that something?

Tiny bones in your cheek, smashed, went fluid. Dumbstruck, you were pissed
by the sour taint of your sad, sputtered imploring. That something

you thought God was supposed to do for you wasn't this—your neck
slamming shut for its own safety. You were a man. That, something

else, and something other were whupped straight out of you that evening,
whizzing cudgels answered and answered when you swore that something

your swagger said that morning should still apply. All you wanted
was to find your feet and stand up. And you prayed that that something

curling orange on the horizon would be fit to breathe, because
you'd rather burn than die cowering, clobbered flat, a numb king.

2

It's no surprise that you coveted the water—born, as you
were, up to your neck in fuel. We wished we could undo that night—

your ragged floodlit flail and swell, bulge of bone, all those scars of
incendiary art. Roadside Jesus, all you knew that night

were ways to turn and turn the other mangled cheek. You gave them
no choice but to heft the cross. You were pummeled blood-blue that night,

then looped and relooped for moral while brick buildings took on ghost,
and mamas howled and clawed their babies' naps for ash. You, that night,

were wick, and your city was a heinous grin, a hard-struck match.
It took all those years to shush your fume. Yes, you lived through that night,

but dreamed of plunging into a blameless cool, your hot head sick
with steam, a cheap tarnished crown bobbing—at last—into the light.

Black, Poured Directly into the Wound

a double golden shovel

Prairie winds blaze through her belly, and Emmett's
red leaving won't name Mamie any kind of mother.
A round-faced sugar whistler, her gone boy is
(through the stiff-clenched mouth of remembering) a
grayed and shadows child. *Listen.* She used to be pretty.
Windy days blasted her skin sweet. She was slight, brown-faced,
in every wide way the opposite of the raw, screeching thing
loss made use of. Now, folded so small, she tires of the
sorries, the *Lawd have mercies.* Grief's damnable tint
is everywhere, darkening days she is no longer aware of.

She is wrong-worshipped, repeatedly emptied of light, pulled
and caressed, cooed at by strangers, offered pork and taffy.
Boys stare hard at her, then snatch back their glares, as if she
killed them too, shipped them to the clutches of South. She sits,
her chair balanced on a grave's edge, and strains for sanity in
kisses upon the imagined cheek of her son. Beginning with *A,*
she recites (*angry, away*) the alphabet of a world gone red.
Coffee sears her throat as church ladies drift about her room,
black garb soaking their hips. They fill cups with water, drinking,
drinking in glimpses of her undoing. The absence of a black

roomful of boy is measured, again. Under the sway of coffee,
red-eyed Mamie knows their well-meaning murmur: *She
a mama, still. You got a chile, you always a mama.* Kisses
in multitudes rain from their Baptist mouths, drowning her.
Sit still, she thinks, *'til they remember how your boy was killed.*

She remembers. *Gush and implosion, crush, slippery, not boy.*
Taffeta and hymns all these women know, not a son lost and
pulled from the Tallahatchie's wretched slog. Mamie, she
of the hollowed womb, is nobody's mama anymore. She is
tinted barren. Everything about her makes the sound *sorry.*

The man-hands on her child, that dangled eye, night chaos,
things that she leans on, the only doors that open to let her in.
Faced with days and days of no him, she lets Chicago—windy,
pretty in the ways of the North—console her with boorish grays,
a stream of mourners and platters of meat to pull her through.
Is this how the backhand slap of sorrow changes the shape of a
mother? Every boy she sees now is laughing, drenched in red.
Emmett whispers *Mama, I am gold.* His bones bless the prairie.

No Wound of Exit

My only sin . . . is in my skin
What did I do . . . to be so black and blue
    —"What Did I Do (To Be So Black and Blue)," recorded by
       Louis Armstrong, 1929

The body is secured in a blue body bag with Medical examiner seal 0000517.

Along with him inside the crackling bag are moonlight, shriek and the entitled groan of vermin. The child was never not secured, but was never secure. He was not apprised of the dangers inherent in the moving forward, so his traipse was conjured of averted gaze, perhaps a rapper's lisp and the spit called rain. The grit of neon sugar works ravage behind his closed mouth. The body is secured in a blue body bag. The body is secured in a blues body bag. The body was crafted to absorb the blues.

The body is viewed unclothed. The body is that of a normally developed black male appearing the stated age of 17 years with a body length of 71 inches and body weight of 158 pounds. The body presents a medium build with average nutrition, normal hydration and good preservation.

(Pause for the definition of a normally developed black male. Avoid the words *tomorrow* and *upright*.)

Rigor mortis is complete, and lividity is well developed and fixed on the posterior surfaces of the body. The body is cold to the touch post refrigeration. Short black hair covers the scalp. The face is unremarkable.

The black face so easily turns a given name to knives. It gobbles questionable meat drenched in red heat and hawks the slick black seeds of melons. It has yawning antebellum pleats and is never ever dark enough for newspapers. Its dance craze is the perp walk, its favorite hangout is above the fold. It squints in a flashlight's probing shriek and slowly, oh so slowly repeats its name. It chats in rebellion reverb. It chats in stereotypical. It is not at all dressed correctly for the job interview. It pants a harried onyx in the bushes behind your duplex. It was designed specifically to identify and reverse your wife. It can no longer hurt you. This particular face, markedly unremarkable, is still baby, not yet terrible with veined big-eye and buck muscle. There's no chance it will fit around your throat. The tree-lined suburb in your chest is safe for now.

There are no fractures, deformities or amputations. The external genitalia present descended testicles and an unremarkable penis. The buttocks are atraumatic, and the anus is intact.

Once, a buyer would gingerly handle the penis of a potential purchase, foraging for heft, for hints of tree trunk, for a commercial cotton foreskin, for its ability to spew a slick black seed.

But dead cancels commerce.

Anus intact? *Sigh.* The ass of the dead boy was rigorously examined after closing hours. One of the thousands of things gingerly removed from its depths was the steamy, jack-booted foot of Florida.

The entrance wound is located on the left chest, 17 1/2 inches below the top of the head, 1 inch to the left of the anterior midline, and 1/2 inch below the nipple.

Further examination demonstrates the wound track passes directly from front to back and enters the pleural cavity with perforations of the left anterior fifth intercostal space, pericardial sac, right ventricle of the heart, and the right lower lobe of the lung.

There is no wound of exit.

A black boy can fold his whole tired self around a bullet. The cartridge is a pinpoint of want, a textbook example of the smallest love. Some slugs are warmer than mothers. The bullet wants the whole of the boy, his snot and insomnia, his crammed pockets and waning current. The bullet strains to romance the blooded one in a way that grinds with lyric. The bullet swoons through his collapsing map, then comes to rest and the boy simply ends his breathing around it. It does not matter if the boy has a mother. It does not matter if he has a gold mouth.

Injuries associated with the entrance wound: perforations of left anterior fifth intercostal space, pericardial sac, right ventricle of the heart, right lower lobe of the lung with approximately 1300 milliliters of blood in the right pleural cavity and 1000 in the left pleural cavity. The collapse of both lungs.

A black boy's lungs collapsing.

A mother picking up a phone.

The same sound.

Incendiary Art: Tulsa, 1921

1

I am a colored boy and you are a white girl. We are in an elevator. Maybe
the elevator goes up, then down, or doesn't. When the doors open you have
already screamed. I am seen running. I do not run, but I am seen running. You
are seen breathy blonde dishevel. I am Dick Rowland and you are Sarah Page.
I am Dick and you are Sarah. I am dick and you are Sarah. I am dick and you
are vessel. You scream and I do not run, but I am seen running. That is the first
end, the fire to everything.

I rub black gleam on white shoes. You run the elevator, hundreds of ups
and downs. Maybe, they say, that's the way you know me, the necessary of up.
The only bathroom for Negroes is on the top floor. I say maybe you know me
another way in those seconds it takes for the rise, my mouth open on the rose
ache of your throat, the dark me spilling on you. Maybe I have entered you,
frantic and upright. Your arms are wrong love, a lucid noose. We crush our
kisses in sync with the elevator's drop and lift. Our shameful clock knows
how little time it takes to spark mayhem in the body. Your scream was that
knowing. My run was that scream.

The definition of love is not this, and all of this anyway. No one believes that
I didn't crack you open and drink. The myriad possible of my black mouth.
A mouth that makes men scurry for twine, religion, torch. A mouth that
made you gasp. And they roar, because they have sniffed my gorgeous neck,
my sweat-crusted neck, my resplendent neck, my impatient neck, my breath
in the ring, and they have dreamed their dream of its length, stretched it all
the way from gasping to the lip of a grave. I hear them beneath me now,
burning their way up, so giddy they almost sing my name. Somewhere, a
branch droops, already weary with me.

2

Sarah, speak to them of the black mouth.
Tell them how a scream
is tumult rudely spilling the borders
of body, tell them
it was
a head snapped back
in hysteria. Make sure they know

how painful

it would have been

to stop

3

They are at their hysterical work, their
hot murders. In my window, I am numb
witness to what bullets shuck. Sarah,
all that inane in our bellies. All that
cursory flail and crush. All
that. Now, all that death beneath
the leaden weight of a sky dragged
dumb by fire. I smell the brick's lazed
succumb, I smell money, I smell a town's whole
skin, singed bald and rising.
Bullets smack flat into
bodies seen running. And then
I smell three hundred
silences, all my crime, all that
cadence stunned
in my name.

See What Happen When You Don't Be Careful

Mama, I knew you didn't mean *maybe* when your blunt
nails dug into the shield of my shoulder. I squared, willed
the muscle hard. *C'mon, girl!* you grunted, reclutching

that shoulder, forcing me, terrified, through the tight knot
of mourning, through the scary squeal of organ, toward that
thing. *C'mon here, girl!*, your big fist raised behind each word,

you tugged hard, dousing me with peppermint spit, but I
vowed root in the sour carpet. When I lifted my head
to find your eyes, roiling, loopy under half-closed lids,

the whites were thin-threaded with raging. Any second
you would lash out in the Lord's name, and He would give you
permission to whip me into dazed surrender toward

the coffin, balanced on its altar in a filtered
blast of stained glass. Just as long as I didn't reach it,
didn't let you wrench or knock me forward that far, it

could be empty. There didn't need to be a reason
for Tony, who everybody called *that sissy*, to
get all of a sudden touched, all sizzle and divine

on that organ, oil-sopped curls flung back, skinny fingers
blazedragging the keys, pushing dangerous deep into
some sneaky ol' resurrection groove. Old hands flap-clapped,

Good Books flew and the funky gut of a hymn bumped blood
thin. I'm so sorry I fought you like a man, Mama,
twisting from you again, my whimpered *I don't wanna*

turning into the grunted *Mama, I ain't gonna,*
and you treated that *ain't* just like I figured you would,
teeth clenched tight, bullet eye, the hauling, three dull dry roads

on the back of my hand where you fought against loosing.
Mama, sorry I made you make a fool of yourself
in front of your God and Rev Thomas and the dry

ancient deacons, I'm sorry you had to slap me hard
on the back of my head to make me open my eyes
until I was face to face with that thing, that thing I

used to call Willie, that sneaky boy who wooed me once
with all of his tongue, who flung little stones to sting my
ankles, who couldn't keep burrs out of his nappy head.

You hustled me right up on all that bright horrible,
that thing now black-bluish chill, put to his last bed on
puffed silk already stinking like shred, both lips blown big

and mistaken rose, my very first dead boy, and you,
Mama, staccato *Look at him, look at him, look at
him,* hurtful with no love and all the love in the words,

in the sound, *Look at him, go on, look!,* the swelling song
of you and the church and Tony, his sissy soul all
knotted and driven, I'm sorry I didn't feel your

frightened heart quivering in your palm on my shoulder
or see the word *mother* setting fire to every day
beyond the day we were standing in, fighting in, in.

Mammy Two-Shoes, Rightful Owner of Tom, Addresses the Lady of the House

Mammy Two Shoes, a character in MGM's "Tom and Jerry" cartoons, was a corpulent, achingly stereotypical black woman seen only from the knees down.

I am double negative charm, carrying the syrupy burden
of your love in my yawning breaches of body. When I laugh,
the sound is a knotted oil on each breath I draw, my lips
spread wide so you can see that my canines are obediently
filed flat—without an evident engine, my bite is no threat
to you or the lily-spiced skin of your throat. I stammer, spurt
submission and rewind, suppressing venom beneath what I'm
sure you have forgotten is an African tongue. I am master

of the google eye, manage vex and fluster when confronted
with your chirping wisdoms. I throw up my buttered
hands in surprise and joy whenever you choose to say my
given name. For the godsend of shelter and food you barely
remember not to throw away, you expect me to be a sexless
stovetop stinking of cinnamon and fat. You don't tell anyone
how inconveniently black I can be, how you have to bolt my
ghost to the kitchen floor so you can find me in the morning.

I'm only simpleminded

on cue. I have hidden in the dry dark of the pantry, weeping,
twisting the light from my fist to keep from striking you. I have
plunged chunks of bread into leaping grease and crammed
my mouth away from exploding. You believe that *yes* is the all
of my language, that I am conjured entirely of bulbous glare

and the head sag, forever on the verge of a grand gospel weep.
You want to believe that I believe that a merciful God laid me
at your feet. But there are days I feel my heart from my knees

to the tile, thudding through calves as thick as the trunks of trees,
calves kissed by the scalloped hem of a daisied apron. My chapped
heels overflow my shoes so I walk as if I was being dragged—
so, so much easier on the sole. And how many times should I
bless you for blessing me, missus, with that tomcat, scheming,
skanked and feral, flea-munched, out of his mind with motivation
and mange, how many ways can I thank you for pushing
a cat into the space where any other woman's child would be?

You gave me that look-down, a feisty relationship with the floor,
permission to wag my flabby finger at something, a little push-pull
oh no you didn't kingdom to rule, an official reason to flap my
gums and call and call on Jesus. I say *Tom, you'se in dat icebox . . .*
you best start to prayin'! I screech *Lawd, lawd, Thomas, is dat*
a mouse? And just like that, I'm up on a quivery dinette chair,
a chair bound to collapse with my overload, everything about
me a'jiggle, my eyes stunned like they been slapped from behind.

In twenty years, you've given me pussy and vermin, the same way
you gave me your squirming, babbling cornsilk-crowned boys, who
started their lives by scarring my breast with their blunt new teeth,
who climbed my body and rode every weary surface that
would hold them. Their stubby fingers gloppy with jelly and snot,
they pried beneath my headrag for the mystery of my hair,
scraped my forearm and cheek raw and looked for black
to be that something alive beneath their nails, and yes, they've slowly

gone stupid with the sugar, lard and mouse droppings I shovel into
their bowls, then into their mouths. And I smile. I slip a tiny razor
into the space between my teeth and the wall of my cheek, and I
smile. At night, after I loudly thank God for the each of you, I never

sleep. I shamble along the floorboards, the nosy cat licking my heels, that mouse skittering blue beneath the stove. Sleep threatens, but I'm careful not to swallow. Just outside your door, I listen to the capture and unlatch of your breath. I move the blade to my resting tongue.

Again, I moan *Yes* and

God says

Don't

Incendiary Art: Ferguson, 2014

they should have
left him there
to be the center
of his own altar,
shat upon, he would have flowered,
his empty hands tucked, ass upended
like a newborn
the lengthy streak of browning
blood could be a sanctified walkway
for the church ladies
for the pokers with their sticks
for the lawbreakers and abiders
for that new kinda worship

they should have
taken advantage of those
fourteen thousand
four hundred seconds and thought
it over for fourteen thousand
more
how sobering it would be
breathless icon as traffic circle
every day
Chevys and livery cabs inching
around the stain
of him   shriekers on the school bus
tasting his blossoming funk
in their clothes
having long ago given up
counting
flies

they should have
left his body
steaming on the asphalt
while passenger-side doors
wrenched from '80s sedans,
flaming barrels of garbage,
charred shards of drugstore,
and bare-chested boys, beautiful
and bulls-eyed,
blurred past in tribute

black lives
matter
most when they are in
motion, the hurtle and reverb
matter   the rushed melody of fist
the shudderings of a scorched
throat matter
the engine that moves us
toward
each damnable dawn
matters

they should have
left him there
as proof

eventually the embers would
have died
in his hair

XXXL

We've lost them all beneath those swaddling clothes.
Cavernous sweats and denims droop with air
and hide our loves inside. They strike the pose,

they cue the swagger, everybody knows
they think they're men. And yet they're wrapped with care.
We've lost them all beneath those swaddling clothes.

Inside, their bodies shudder, come to blows
with time. Their fractured lives can't reach them there.
Love hides inside. They coil, they strike. The pose,

if it is done just right, wards off the blows
that real men can see coming. Say a prayer.
We've lost them all beneath their swaddling clothes.

They've chosen this dull way to drown. That shows
it really doesn't matter that we care,
they must hide love inside. They strike the pose

of men because, as we have come to know,
no babies strut these streets—they wouldn't dare.
We've lost them all beneath their swaddling clothes.
They hide our love inside, then strike the pose.

Emmett Till: Choose Your Own Adventure

Turn to page 48 if Emmett Till's body is never found.

Our chubby grinner, just another child
who ambled into mist, no tip or trace,
no signs that he was hunted or reviled
before he turned into a jagged space
that wasn't there, then was. Nobody saw
that city boy whose swagger marked him first
as clueless, then as fool. Into the maw
of Mississippi at its very worst,
he disappeared without a single sound—
no screech or mannish giggle, wounded cry
or whistle. Mama Mamie, counting down
to zero, grasped the hands of passersby—
the white ones muttered *Girl, leave us alone.*
The Negroes said *You should have left him home.*

How to Bust into a Black Man's House and Take a Boy Out

Do not be frightened
of the threshold. Do not
be withered by the fact
that the black man's
mama named him Moses.
Jesus is no willing witness
to this. The boy will be
asleep.

II

WHEN BLACK MEN DROWN THEIR DAUGHTERS

Nobody wanted your dance,
Nobody wanted your strange glitter, your floundering
Drowning life and your effort to save yourself,
Treading water, dancing the dark turmoil,
Looking for something to give.
  —Ted Hughes, "God Help the Wolf after Whom
    the Dogs Do Not Bark"

In February 2010, 21-year-old student Shamshiddin Abdur-Raheem abducted his 3-month-old daughter Zara. He placed her in a knapsack, drove to a bridge on the Garden State Parkway in New Jersey and threw her out of the passenger-side window of his car. She drowned in the Raritan River, more than 100 feet below.

In November 2011, also in New Jersey, Arthur Morgan III picked up his 2-year-old daughter Tierra for a trip to the movies. Later, Tierra was found facedown in a frigid stream beneath a park overpass, strapped into a car seat which had been weighed down with a car jack. It was unclear whether she was thrown from the overpass or carried into the park and placed in the water.

1
The Five Stages of Drowning

Surprise

There is no drunk like the drunk of milk sleep.
A drizzled white floods the body and weighs down
everywhere we think we know about awake.
Zara's new clockwork staggers with it while Daddy,
grizzle and wild-eye, lobs her like trash over
the rusting rail. Inside the sack, the wriggling child
cannot translate *fly, plummet, descend.* She doesn't
realize the hard questions she poses for pigeons
or how, so dull and stupid with dairy, she is all
the fall the sky can language. Babies accept what

they are given. They never question the morning's
flood of sun, a kitchen's blaring stink, or the wide
hovering faces of fathers. After a swollen breeze

pries her eyes open in the few seconds it takes for
the fevered discarding of daughter, baby doesn't
ask the sun, needling light into the sack, to offer
rule or direction. Zara Malani-Lin Abdur-Raheem,
little not-bird, has been jettisoned, ditched, unloaded.
Her snared arms can find no rhyme for *wing*.
The river's glittering trash smacks her blunt,

but not before her tiny O fails its role as mouth,
not before language breaks its promise to wait
for her. If Zara can conjure no word for *word*, can
find no way to bellow *Up, Daddy, up* as she tumbles,
stuffed inside a *downdowndown* reeking so oddly
of him, how would she voice panic born of the day's
quick fist? Slapped awake, she breathes in the close
cloth and feels the little ruckus of a new heart.
The startled river opens, then closes over her, the way
a new mother would.

Involuntary Breath Holding

Imagine filling your whole body with everything you are
and then holding it there. Imagine the smallness of that body.

You are nothing but the easy of blue, red and green, food
you have smashed with your fingers, and the stumbling

possibilities of walk. Imagine not knowing that the ability
to contain all of you in tiny ballooned cheeks decides whether

you continue. Imagine not knowing the word *continue*.
Quick wisps of fish nip warily at those fat cheeks, fall into

irreparable love and decide to make a new religion of you.
Hallelujah, you are now a religion, a church of slither and slide

while Daddy roars his glee into noontime traffic, not thinking
about you, but thinking about your mother, and screeching *Oh, she*

got another man now, huh? Well, fuck that ho, I got sumthin
for her ass! Bet this gon' fix her bitch ass now, and you, Tierra,

are the fix for her ass now, you are the fix for Mama's ass now,
you are the pawn in a payback that *cannot* be unplayed. And

your daddy, now miles away from your slow plunging, does a lousy
parking job and stumbles into a smoky, red-walled gin mill

populated by other men without daughters. Hoisting a fat gold
shot, he toasts his one accomplishment—the uncomplicated

removal of a complication—while your cheeks deflate and the door
to your next minute closes. You were alive when the stream first

lapped its way 'round you, and the *d* sound comes so sweet to
the mouth of a baby who wants it. You laughed *D-Daddy* until

the giddy fish reexamined their worship of you, you coughed
Daddy Daddy until *Daddy Daddy* was nothing but sound,

then you spat *d d d* into the mud until you couldn't. The fickle
fish, back in love, kissed the place where your breath had been.

Hypoxic Convulsions

Daddy is the architect of a baby girl's roll and rock.
He teaches her to manage slink, schools her in a woman's
wet engine. If Zara lives—which she most definitely
will not—
somebody else's daddy will teach her all the one way
there is not to get lured into a sack, how to lay quietly

in the wrong skirt while her muscles argue,
how one well-timed convulsion
usually clears the dance floor. Like good drowning,
good dancing hits the backside like an annoyance
that must be watusied loose. But how to respond
to a sudden wet that's out to rearrange? Of course—
drums are injected—
and Tierra, all thrash and snapdragon,
shimmies for her giggle back. Baby is the battery
black women build their bodies around
until they're old enough to be officially romanced
by yet another revision of Jesus. But right now

they're too little to feel the full hand
of the Jesus voice, the caress of proverb and psalm.
They're flirting with that Big Daddy for all their
little worth—look at that itty jerk and boogaloo,
that pop swirling of hips they can't find, that runaway
rimshot in unfinished chests. They're rearing back,
opening wide,
rearing back, opening
wide, rearing
back, both throats
opening and slamming
shut with river.

Cue the skanky music. Brackish water snags
the rhythm, controls their arms and ankles,
gleefully involves their necks, it says

Baby,
save the last dance
for me.

Unconsciousness

The river, tho. Sluggish and cagey and habitually a bitch,
she has not decided to accept Zara, this vexation in her mouth.
She is dazzled by choke, flopped blossoms and the occasional
seduced diver, but repulsed by all frailties of skin. The river
is seldom in a mood to have her swerve scrutinized or interrupted.
Now what is this damned hindrance, keeling over in the current?
Prying the sack wide with gush, she prods the puckered contents,
is *not* entertained. Intending to add the ugly pudge to her baubles,
she finds that she cannot rouse it, is *so* not entertained. The little
blue not-fish thing is flaccid, so unfun, snazzed up in its sopping
petal pink, the eyes slit and rolling, nappy crown trapping living
things that desperately need to breathe. The hide skids and burps.
The river's most devoted feeders, so jazzed at first, have already
had a go at it. And the thing won't give the river its props, won't
beg for refuge in the water's arms, it won't *say* anything. The river
flicks a bored blue finger at it, then flicks it away. She is so *over*
this drama. Hell, the end of anything is only a kick to watch once.

Clinical Death

> The final stage in the drowning process is death. Clinical death
> occurs when both breathing and circulation stop. The victim
> is in cardiac arrest. The heart stops pumping blood. The vital
> organs are no longer receiving oxygen-rich blood. The lack of
> oxygen causes the skin to turn blue.

There are 52 shades of blue—or a million and 52, depending upon which river
you ask.

  3: Cornflower.

17: Cerulean.

21: Blunt force.

28: Turquoise.

34: Navy.

37: *Fix for her bitch ass now.*

41: Sky.

47: *Goodbye*—but the way the river says it: *"Bye"*—all dismissal and shade.

52: *Goodbye*—but the way a daddy says it—over his shoulder, thrilling
the done of the deed,
already mad
at the traffic.

2
Sentencing

In November 2012, Shamsiddin Abdur-Raheem, 24, was
sentenced to life in state prison for murdering Zara, plus an
additional 30 years to be served consecutively for kidnapping
her. He told the judge that he often wondered what his daughter
would have looked like, and what she could have done.

She would have wept her life to its outer edges,
after misunderstanding so much:

The first time a man soft-swept the underside
of her chin with just the right verb.

The yawning vessels of blood, linked hard
to the tides, controlling the conceits of her body.

How she sang incessantly of fathers,
their pinprick beards. Their wide cars.

She would have looked like: A wound beginning to close.
What she could have done:

In May 2014, Arthur Morgan III, 29, charged with the murder of his 2-year-old daughter Tierra, was sentenced to life in prison without the possibility of parole. Before sentencing, he bemoaned the end of his relationship with the child's mother, but never apologized for murdering Tierra.

In those first giddy, rampaging stages of fool-for-love,
it's impossible to see that untethering in the eye.
Even as she vowed before multitudes in her glass dress,
she couldn't know how keenly he would define devotion.
Soon they tangled hard. A whole white kitchen shattered,
and he screeched that he would die before he let another
man open his mouth upon her braids or bite good into
the roped muscle of her bare shoulder. Once he renamed her,
she clawed through her half-life, steady fixed on a horizon
that wobbled and strayed. Giggling whenever a door slammed,
the baby couldn't help sporting the nose of her father.
She cooed contentedly through her doomed days, spelling *Daddy*
with plump, jelly-glopped fingers, and that's how he knew
she'd be the utterly perfect fix for her mother's ass now.

Why the Verdict Just Don't Sound Right; or, The Bobbing Baby Blues

Every song has a finish, a twanged coda siphoned
of every tint but blue. Organ is woefully underused.
An Alabama woman plucks a shining revolver from
a box in her chest. Or moral is slammed home by
a stooped, colicky elder with a one-syllable sickness
for a name. By the time the lights come up, the stage
is noxious with sweat. All night long, no one could
carry the tune because it was just so damned heavy.

A man, whose flat American name was long ago pushed
aside by the snarling melodics of Allah, lobbed his baby
over the rail of a bridge into the arms of a pissed river
where she eddied and sank. Another man, lewd-laughing
with his wide mouth, strapped iron across his daughter's
twitching chest and rejoiced as she fought for air with her
arms. On separate days, years apart, their gaping sin was
recounted while a childless woman wailed in backdrop.
And although they both bowed their heads on cue (only
one at the explicit angle of shame), although each had
diligently schooled his left eye in the staccato jerk
of the unhinged, although they'd donned crisp suits
and shiny whiteboy loafers, they were found guilty.
Even court-scrubbed and cuffed, their hands stank
of flung daughters. The last thing both men heard
was one blue note, dangerously off-key, as it unreeled
up, cracking and saturnine from the river's throat.

Outwardly divine, the river's skin is a tricky meld
of crystal and trash. Just beneath it, miserable legions
of rickety crooners teach her how to mourn. They snivel
and wail, blasting their hearts through their harps, steady
threatening *Baby, if you don't do right* to end it all.

3

This is no movie.
In cinematic oceans, white people flail,
pray upward,
shop for late-breaking religions.
Their histories trail listlessly
behind them as credits roll. But here
in Jersey, we go hard.
No otherworldly light,
no storyline beyond this.

4

On every inch of me, there are rumors of fathers,
all of them stifling snarls
behind the grinning death mask
of the one who gave me name.

Stubbled and siren, they have scrubbed me
seriously clean of hair,
pummeled my weight,
wrenched my adoring breath
from its moorings.

Slyly, they measure the shrinking distance
between me
and the water.

5
Meanwhile, the Mother

wrangles the instance over and over, the moment when
her man (she has no other way of naming him, even after)
reached out for their baby daughter 'til her fingers fell from
the baby's arm and all that wild, wriggling weight was his.
She still smells the honeyed talcum and sweet oil flowering
the child's skin, the soured underline of that morning's belched milk.
The high-tops, tersely bowed, were thick-swiped with chalky polish,
and that damned plait had snaked loose again, popping the knot
in the striped ribbon. The baby, noting the coos on edge, did
her wide-eyed glisten weep through a stupefied smile. Daddy's
teeth were bared as he asked for his daughter's scalloped-hem coat
to keep her cozy against the wind, warm for the wet kill.
While the mother watched him fold a tiny arm and push it
into a sleeve, she wanted to say to the child *Sometimes*
a love is like this but before she could, a door flew wide
and the sun surged, blasting the man and his burden into
shade. The daughter flapped fingers goodbye and burbled one last
glee the mother needed to hear as a word. It wasn't.

When Black Men Drown Their Daughters

When black, men drown. They spend their whole lifetimes
justifying the gall of springing the trap, the inconvenience
of slouched denim, of coupling beyond romance or aim.
All the while, the rising murk edges toward their chins.
Hurriedly, someone crafts another scientific tome, a giddy
exploration of the curious dysfunction identifying black
men first as possible, then as necessary. Elegant equations
succumb to a river that blurs quotient and theory, rendering
them unreadable, and the overwhelm easily disappears
the men, their wiry heads glistening, then gulped. All that's
left is the fathers' last wisdom, soaked wreckage on silver:
Girl, that water ain't nothing but wet. I'm gon' be alright.

When black men drown, their daughters turn to their mothers
and ask *What should I do with this misnamed shiver in my
left shoulder? How should I dress in public?* They are weary
of standing at the shore, hands shading their eyes, trying
to make out their own fathers among the thousands bobbing
in the current. The mothers mumble and point to any flailing
that seems familiar. Mostly, they're wrong. Buoyed by church
moans and comfort food of meat and cream, the daughters
try on other names that sound oddly broken when pressed
against the dank syllables of the fathers'. Drained, with just
forward in mind, they walk using the hip of only one parent.
They scratch in their sleep. Black water wells up in the wound.

When black men drown, their daughters are fascinated with
the politics of water, how gorgeously a surface breaks
to receive, how it weeps so sanely shut. And the thrashing
of hands, shrieking of names: *I was Otis, I was Willie Earl,
they called me Catfish.* Obsessed by the waltzing of tides,

the daughters remember their fathers—the scorch of beard
electrifying the once-in-a-while kiss, the welts in thick arms,
eyes wearied with so many of the same days wedged behind
them. When black men drown, their daughters memorize all
the steps involved in the deluge. They know how long it takes
for a weakened man to dissolve. A muted light, in the shape
of a little girl, used to be enough to light a daddy's way home.

When black men drown, their daughters drag the water's floor
with rotting nets, pull in whatever still breathes. They insist their
still-dripping daddies sit down for cups of insanely sweetened
tea, sniffs of rotgut, tangled dinners based on improbable swine.
The girls hope to reacquaint their drowned fathers with the concept
of body, but outlines slosh in drift and retreat. The men can't get
dry. Parched, they scrub flooded hollows and weep for water
to give them name and measure as mere blood once did. Knocking
over those spindly-legged dinette chairs, they interrupt the failed
feast and mutter *Baby girl, gotta go, baby gotta go,* their eyes
misted with their own murders. Grabbing their girls, they spit
out love in reverse and stumble toward the banks of some river.

When black men drown their daughters, the rash act is the only
plausible response to the brain's tenacious mouth and its dare: *Yes,
yes, open your ashed hands and release that wingless child.* Note
the arc of the sun-drenched nosedive, the first syllable of the child's
name unwilling from the man's mouth, the melody of billow that
begins as blessed clutch. Someone crouching inside the father waits
impatiently for the shutting, the lethargic envelop, and wonders if
the daughter's wide and realizing eye will ever close to loose him.
It never will, and the man and his child and the daughter and her
father gaze calmly into the wrecked science of each other's lives.
The sun struggles to spit a perfect gold upon the quieting splash.
The river pulses stylish circles of its filth around the swallow.

Blurred Quotient and Theory

My mother and father fought like there was one
breath in the room and only one throat could have
it. They fought like Crisco and a scarlet skillet,
like cold hose-spray fights with cats coupling
in a night alley. All day they walked gingerly on
their raised fists, all night she played 'bama pure
until Otis Redding lit their hips and nasty flecks
of old tobacco flowed from his gold tooth to hers.
They spat backwood, each one craving all the South
in the other. One of them regretted me. And it was
that one who fixed her mouth to say *Get on outta*
here, Otis, and after that my father lived in one place

and me in another. All my friends who were girls
had a father living in one place while they lived
in another, and if you were a girl, that was alright.
Girls needed their mamas. *There my daddy go right*
there was the chime, with a fingerpoint at the corner
store, at a passenger-side rider in a passing Buick,
at a smoky figure slipping into some other door,
at a worker swinging his lunch bucket, at a hooter
in sharkskin whistling at somebody else's mama,
at a man getting his face slapped with cologne after
a haircut, at a dice game winner in Garfield Park,
and sometimes this sadness: *Well, I* think *that's him.*

Sometimes a daughter is simply what the middle
of a crib does. Later, she becomes the opener
of doors. She warms that plate of neckbones,
and pirouettes for his gaze. Sometimes she is the spit

of the mother, the irritant prancing the outer edge
of rooms, the cheek roughly pinched, the handful
of dimes and *Go on, get yourself some Red Hots,*
the math problem one person in class keeps getting
wrong, the *Sit on in here and be still while your mama
and I*—Sometimes she is sometimes. She is an oddity,
or she is air. What Tierra was was shatter to anyone
doomed enough to love her. What Zara was was not a son.

III

ACCIDENTAL

How simple a thing it seems to me that to know ourselves
as we are, we must know our mothers' names.
—Alice Walker, *O: The Oprah Magazine*, May 2003

Sagas of the Accidental Saint

For the mothers of the lost

I don't expect you'll recognize my voice.
I don't believe this saga I've suppressed
will ever sound familiar. I am just

a stooped and accidental saint, no choice
except to strain the limits of my throat.
I am the mama weep beneath the fold,

that paragraph you skip, the wink of gold
inside a rotted mouth, that shredding note
of grief. Excuse what's inexcusable

in me—the shifting wildfire-tinted weave,
my ankles blue with fluid, how I grieve
in gospel you can't clutch—a fusible

display of doubled negatives I spew
whenever someone says my child is gone
and then goes on to pile the blame upon

my child for being gone. Or maybe you
believe the wretched mess is rightly traced
right back to *me,* whose body housed the crime—

my daughter out of dollars, out of time,
my son just seeking ways to be erased.
So many ways they stride into the line

of gunfire, tease the trigger, crave the shot,
just living through their days as if they're not
about to die. He totes a paper bag of wine,

or tussles, laughing, with his kid or rolls
a joint or asks his boo to braid his hair
while lazing on the stoop, or dares to glare

when someone shoves. She fights against the holds
around her throat or somehow looks the same
as someone else or sits inside her car

or someone else's car, or leaves ajar
a door she should have closed. He plays a game
of hoops to clear his head, or doesn't raise

his hands, or raises them, or doesn't stop
or does, or, when commanded, fails to drop
his wallet, keys or phone. He sets ablaze

a heap of trash, somebody's car or store,
while shouting slogans meant to make you care
that he's alive. She's killed if she's not there

although she said she'd be, or there before
she should have been, or on her way to work,
or coming home not walking like she should,

not walking down the street she normally would.
He walks too close behind, you have to jerk
your purse out of the way, you palm the mace,

he passes, spitting lyric vile and blue,
not giving damns that he's offending you.
All you can remember is his race.

You ask him to succumb, he dares decline,
the situation quickly falls apart.
A weapon's raised to line up with his heart

because he feels entitled to his spine.
She fumbles in her pocket for some change
or jumps the A train turnstile on a dare.

She mumbles like her mind is not all there,
or titters in a way you think is strange.
He wrecks his Chevy, waves for help, he calls

the 9 the 1, the 1. He's *waiting* wrong,
the folks around him said he didn't belong.
He coughs or sneezes, looks away, he brawls

with brothers, sisters, father, wife. He waves
a Walmart toy, or he can't find his place
in line, he laughs too loud, he can't retrace

his steps, he droops his pants, he misbehaves.
She turns her back or whirls around or could
be packin', could be wanted, could be strong

enough to snap your neck. She moves all wrong.
He wanders into someone else's hood
in colors that he struggles to explain.

He prances, strides, he's plotting an escape,
he stops and spins on you, he's here to rape
your daughter. Or he scoffs when you complain

about his smell, he crafts a sign, he parks
behind your Chevy, thrusts his massive fist
into or through the air, he wakes up pissed

but right on time, then smokes a blunt or arcs
his brow when someone asks *You good?* He waits
his turn or takes a break, he takes a leak,

he frightens everyone with his physique,
the situation's bound to escalate.
So many ways they're asking not to be.

She's wearing out her welcome, being black
when no one's asked her to, you've seen her lack
of grace, the space she occupies, her glee

when chicken, weed or welfare checks roll in.
He goes to class, he graduates, he takes
the seat right next to you, his shoulder makes

you quake inside. You simply don't know when
he'll blow. She shops beneath the winking eye
of video, but then pays with a card

that *can't* be hers. His chest and arms are scarred
with scrape and blood tattoos—so why untie
the noose shaped like his neck? His clothes are blue

or red, he wants your job, he's scoped your wife,
he craves your home, your cash, your perfect life,
that textbook in his hand's not fooling you.

She hawks and spits, she begs for change, she blows
a harp, she blows through blow, she blows her chance,
a victim, yet again, of circumstance.

He's fighting back, but everybody knows
that he's too coarse, too dumb, too street, too black,
too dense, too doomed, too thick, too much of those,

too vicious pose, too quick to come to blows,
too likely he could spark your heart attack.
He flares his nostrils, hides his hands, he flees

without explaining why. She lifts, she steals,
she swipes, she grabs, she snatches, cuts a deal.
He stumbles, trips, he trips a wire, he sees

too much, she needs too much, he feels too much,
her skin's too mud, his skin's too light, he fights
too dirty, fights for breath, the savage nights

are huge with him, the voodoo in his touch—
he shoots himself while handcuffed to a pole,
or hangs himself while hanging from a tree,

or wrings his neck although his hands aren't free.
He always seems to fail at self-control.
He's monster, ogre, he's the looming threat,

insisting he didn't do that thing he did,
denying that she'd hidden what she hid,
confusing you by getting so upset.

He claims he's innocent, he files a case,
he lives too large, too long, he must believe
that he is white or free. He's so naive—

with every step he takes, he falls from grace.
He steps inside or out, or through or down,
she bellows, jumps or hisses, struts or spins,

he stalks a street, steps off a curb. His sins
should be enough to drive him out of town,
where he'd be out of sight and out of mind

and out of bounds but thankfully not out
of range. And if you think he's all about
the kill, the drops, the guns and gangster grind,

you know for sure as soon as you see me—
his mama, grieving ugly, wailing 'bout
my chile, my chile, and plucking Jesus out

of every bag. You just can't see why he
deserves such stupid love—my wailing thrusts,
each *Lord have mercy on my baby's soul,*

my sad theatrics as my child goes cold.
And then the hungry cameras readjust
my howls—until it's not my child who's dead,

but something feral, edged in leak, a threat
to shrubbery and Sundays. While he's wet
and seeping into street, they frame his head

and mine inside a single shot and ask
my nappy hair and bulging eyes just what
I think. I keen, implode on cue. They cut

the camera back to frame the blooded mask
and splay. You don't remember what I say,
or hear his name, but you are borderline

obsessed with my collapse, my crumpled whine
and holy-ghosted flail, the matinee
of mama. You are entertained until

you aren't. And then I'm just an open maw,
a blur and tongue. You shouldn't waste your awe
on my unleashed display of overkill.

Ignore the blackish bruiser, dripping bile,
the spittle-spewing me, still bellowing
my Lord my Lord why would you let this thing

disrupt your day? I disappear. And while
I'm relegated to an anecdote
on way to nothing, all you can recall

is sputtered gospel woe and caterwaul,
that corpse the tightened wire around my throat.

that's my son collapsed there my son
crumpled there my son lying there
my son positioned there my daughter
repositioned there my daughter as
exhibit A there my daughter dumped
over there my son hidden away there
my son blue there my son dangling
there my son caged there my daughter
on the gurney there on the slab there
in the drawer there my daughter splayed
there my son locked down there my
son hanging there my son bleeding
out there my son growing frigid there
my daughter deposited there my son
inside the chalk there my daughter
being bagged there my son on the slab
there my son crushed there my son
rearranged there my son crumpled
in the door there my daughter's neck
shrinking in the noose there my son's
left eye over there my son as exhibit B
there my son behind the wheel there
my son under the wheels there my son
slumped over the wheel there my son

my daughter blooded and not moving
in the doorway on the stoop down
the block in front of her kids just inside
the barbershop facedown in the street
outside the bodega inside the bodega
in the black alley behind the bodega
on the videotape a block from home
leaving home hanging out at home
in the schoolyard on the blacktop
in his bed in her kitchen in my arms
in my arms in my arms that's my son
shot to look thug that's my daughter
shot to look more animal shot as kill
shot as prey shot as conquest shot as
solution shot as lesson shot as warning
shot as comeback shot as payback shot
for sport shot for history that's my son
not being alive any more there that's my
child coming to rest one layer below
the surface of the

rest

of my life

      there

August 19, 2014, St. Louis, MO— Kajieme Powell, 25, was accused of shoplifting donuts and energy drinks. Police said the mentally disturbed man approached with a knife "in an overhand grip"—they shot him dead 15 seconds after they arrived. Video shows that Powell's hands were at his side.

I am the mother of that darkest magician. His thousand
limbs thrash in and out of your practiced sightline.
He is always behind, beside and in front of you.
He lunges for your neck while whistling on a side street
three blocks away. Firepower throbs in every finger
of his bound or idle hands. No matter where he is,
he is the leading man in the stuttering convenience store video.

If he is not there,

> he will be.

If he hasn't,

> he is about to.

If a blade's not in his hand, it's

> in his hand.

If his hands are up,
they're clawing through his pockets

> for

something.

If he's screeching *Don't shoot!*

> he's clearly saying
> *Please. I'm tired. Help me fall down.*

December 2, 2014, Phoenix AZ— Rumain Brisbon, 34, an unarmed
father of four, was shot to death when a police officer
mistook a bottle of pills for a gun.

The son of the mother of mistake, he was
clearly saying
Please.
I'm tired.
Help me fall down.

Nothing in that bottle could end his
hurting quicker than that one stormy
lyric turning final in his chest.
His hundred fingers were stumblers,
dark and probably. My children
are blasted daily out of their own
names, paying with breath for the sin
of pockets. And wallets. And bottles.
And phones. And toys. Choking on
the iron stench of blood, he reached
for the day after the one he was falling in.
Nothing good was there. Nothing good
ever reached back.

March 3, 2014, Iberia Parish, LA— Police say that Victor White III, 22, shot himself while handcuffed in the back of a police cruiser.

November 19, 2013, Durham, NC— Police say that Jesus Huerta, 17, shot himself while handcuffed in the back of a police cruiser.

July 29, 2012, Jonesboro, AR— Police say that Chavis Carter, 21, shot himself while handcuffed in the back of a police cruiser.

He reached back and found
his own hands with his own
hands, worked his bound
fingers to set his free fingers
loose, then used that shackled
hand to free the other shackled
hand, and the freed shackled
hand, still shackled, was still
bound to the other hand once
both were freed. Once free
in the shackles, the shackled
hands turned to the matter
of the gun, which couldn't be
there because they'd searched
my baby twice and a gun is
a pretty big thing unless it isn't,
unless it is dreamed alive by
hands that believe they are no
longer shackled. Stunned in
cuffs, but free and searching,
the left and right hands found
a gun with a stink like voodoo,

a gun that couldn't have been
there, wasn't there, but was.
The left-handed him used
a cuffed hand, which could
have been either left or right
(since both were free), to root
around for a trigger and fire
a bullet right into his left-
handed head, impossible but
not really, since the preferred
killing hand may have preferred
its shackles. The policemen,
who had searched my baby
twice and cuffed both his free
and unfree hands behind his
back before his hands found
his own hands and pulled,
heard no human sound at all
during all that frantic magic,
no *Fuck!* as my boy struggled
to get his left shackled hand
to do what his right shackled
hand wouldn't do, no frenzied
pound of one bracing foot
against the door, no grunt
or whoop of glee to mark all
all those times he slipped out
of custody and in again. But
they did hear the bang
of the gun that wasn't there
(but was) just when it sent
that bullet into the right side
of his left-handed head. *Sounds
like sacrifice,* they thought.

Slumped, eyes cocked and
undone, my child was amazed
at the sweet hoodoo he had
managed. Both left and right
hands were shackled and free
behind him, there was an eerie
perfect circle of smoke in his
hair. *Suicide,* they both said at
the very same time, and since
it was odd how they had reached
the same conclusion, they smiled
and shook their heads. Noting
the shackles, they praised their
God in the light of miracle while
the boy who couldn't have done
what he did, but did, bled down
to zero. *Guess he couldn't take it,*
one of the alive said to the other.
He didn't mean wearing the shackles.
He meant not wearing them.

March 15, 2012, Queens, NY— Shereese Francis, 30, a schizo-
phrenic, had stopped taking her medications and needed an
ambulance. Police arrived, handcuffed an agitated Shereese,
and held her facedown on a mattress until she went into
cardiac arrest and stopped breathing.

She couldn't get out from under the venom
flooding the muscle across the span of her back,
the command that she *Breathe!* from a growler
with both knees on her breath. She couldn't
summon the spit she needed to call out for me
or debate the hammers taking flower behind
her eyes. With flecks of his spit in her perm
and a prickly pressure suppressing her spine,
maybe she thought that the abrupt theft of beat
was how Jesus ended mayhem in the body—
with all the mayhem at once and then none.
Her life, relived at its end, unreeled as brash
cinema. It was lucid, as bright as backhand:

A pair of patent leather Mary Janes with taps
and gilded buckles. A walk through a hundred
songs with half her heart, all the swerve, all
sugar intact. A laugh with an open mouth. Even
when her mind careened and fled for tumbling
lights, she was my child. She hurtled forward
from my body, and her living was a struggle
to clutch. I loved her beauty. I loved her unkilled.

June 22, 2007, West Memphis, AR— DeAunta Terrell Farrow, 12,
was gunned down by police officer Erik Sammis, who claimed
that only after he shot Farrow did he realize that the gun
the child was carrying was a toy.

Even mamas were 12 once, screeching
glee and unkilled. I skipped in All Stars.
Even girls who became mamas once had
silver toy pistols that spat sparks to startle

the church ladies. We hung plastic handcuffs
from our belts and hurled rock-hard balls
at each other's bellies and heads. There
were knots, sometimes blood, on our lips.

We made our mouths make sounds like
bullets, we dodged fun that was out to break
us. Drunk on that little glee, we murdered
and murdered and murdered each other.

Like Tom, that cartoon cat, we collapsed,
unblooded, our skulls turned completely
around, bulged eyes on the ground by our
heads, our ears blown off. But we got up,

ready to be killed again. Again. We had all
seen Tom shotgunned, knifed, beheaded,
bitten, poisoned, exploded. Once, he was
misled by a cooing puss in a snug skirt,

and his heart broke out right through his
chest. A little surprised every time he died,
but unfazed by his resurrections, he'd brush
it off, reattach his head, lick his paw, smooth

his fur like *That's all you got?* So, like him,
I made a game out of losing and finding my
life. I fell and fell and got back up, corduroys

stiff, knees throbbing with scrape. I sprang
right up, swinging swears, already running
through a lengthy laundry list of vengeance,
every sweet payback ending with *You dead!*

Lay down! Yes, I fell down dead, but I
always popped right back up, maybe a little
closer to dying, but still 12, as certain as
black cats, and, in the end, utterly alive.

That's why I arched over his body, willing
his leaks to seal, praying him into a wacky
and improbable cartoon resurrection,
into *Get up, get up, get up, please get
up,* but then the credits rolled, which meant
the day was fresh out of his brand of breath—

even his color

began to leave.

November 19, 2011, White Plains, NY— The LifeAid medical
alert bracelet of Kenneth Chamberlain Sr., 68, was
triggered by mistake. When the police responded, he refused
to open the door to his apartment, saying he did not need
help. A LifeAid recording captured officer Steven Hart
calling him a "nigger." After working for an hour to
force open the door, the police broke it down, tasered
Chamberlain and shot him dead.

My son was hunched vintage, a nighttime.
You need our help, boy, you need our help.
He placed a finger on his slow-throbbing
neck, knew for a fact that his heart still
knew its right place beneath his shirt.
*You just don't know you need our help, let
us in, let us in.* He couldn't say no enough,
hating the old Negro waver in the word.
*Let us into your gas stove, your couch, your
nasty tousled bed, your rat skittering blue
note behind the trash.* That damned rat, all
the music he had. *Your heart's not right,
you're running a fever, nigger.* Where was he,
Mississippi? Was he a boy, barefoot again,
running wild for no reason, pounding
all that red dust dizzy? Was he on fire
again? *You feel hot through this wood.*

> *We're here to help*
his heart clenched
> *we're here to fall you down*
and the fire walked a road
> *to fall you down*
through my child's body
> *to stop your worry*

and straight up to
   nigger, to fix your life
that moon
   to make it right
he always watched
   to give you rest
and wanted

March 12, 2012, Pasadena, CA— Kendrec McDade, 19, was
chased and shot seven times by two police officers after
a 911 caller falsely reported being robbed at gunpoint
by two black men. McDade's final words were "Why did they
shoot me?"

As the moon tangled its beams and grew
monstrous huge over his body, he wanted
that answer. As usual, I arrived too late—
he had already dispersed, and become an
awkward hour. Son of the mother of mistake,
his timing and root were askew. But

*because walk because upright because Africa because decision because Tuesday
because loaded gun because running because two black because identified because
uniform because breathless because unable because America because yo mama
because Mississippi because uniform because Obama because the chase because
unarmed because convenient because mistaken because threatened because ritual
because no one will miss you because beast because innocent because they could
because they could because they could because they could because they—*

I usually give my boys names anybody can remember.
Scapegoat. Target. PerpWalk. HeDidIt. Oversight.
The name Kendrec so quashed his potential. He should
have been *Victim. Identify. Bullseye. NotAgain.*
Miracle. 2BlackMenWithAGun. How about—

Accident.
Perfect.

I never had children.

I just had accidents.

September 14, 2013, Bradfield Farms, NC— After being involved in a traffic accident, Jonathan Ferrell, 24, knocked on the door of a nearby house for help. The woman inside called the police. They arrived and shot him ten times.

My son said: *I just had an accident. I need to use a phone.*
She said: *You're black.*
My son said: *It'll only take a minute. I need to call the police.*
She heard: *Call the police.*
My son said: *I know it's late, but—I just had an accident.*
She said: *911.*
He said: *OK, then. You'll call 911?*
She said: *You're black.*
The police said: *Is he black?*
She said: *He's black.*
When the gun arrived, it said *I just had an accident.*

The gun said: *I just had an accident.*

The gun said: *I just had an accident.*

The gun said: *I just had an accident.*

The gun said: *I just had an accident.*

The gun said: *I just had an accident.*

The gun said: *I just had an accident.*

The gun said: *I just had an accident.*

The gun said: *I just had an accident.*

The gun said: *I just had an accident.*

March 21, 2012, Chicago, IL— Rekia Boyd, 22, was killed
by off-duty police detective Dante Servin. Saying he saw
someone pull a gun and point it at him, Servin fired five
rounds over his left shoulder, through his car window, into
a crowd. Boyd was struck in the back of the head. The gun
Servin saw was actually a cell phone.

He just had an accident. Every shuffled air
is stumbling and probably. And there was
Rekia, knotted in a black flow that conjured
the idea of army. He smelled them at his back
and knew he would never have survived their
intent with only the thin wall of a car around him.

If they haven't,

                they are about to.   The glint.

If a gun's not in his hand,

                it's in his hand.   The slow

menace of how they meant his end.

If a bullet's not in the barrel   The fierce

                it's in the air   whipping

to nape of neck
to her slow unloosing box braid
to jaw muscle
to the snap of
his New Era fitted,

to Indian Remy
to the spine's sweet tip
to a turned back

                                       you know
sometimes they don't find
the whole head

once it is mist,
it drips from chainlink
seeps into asphalt
clogs storm drains

becomes
too fluid
for me

       to mourn

February 28, 2003, Las Vegas, NV— Orlando Barlow, 28, was
surrendering on his knees in front of four police officers
when one of them shot him with an assault rifle from 50 feet
away. Barlow was unarmed. The officer said he was afraid
that Barlow was faking surrender. Federal investigators
later discovered that the same officers had printed T-shirts
labeled "bdrt," for "Baby Daddy Removal Team."

He obediently folded to his knees, slow-stuttering
Yes sir yes sir yes sir yes sir like I taught him,
sinking deep, kingmaker, his eyes locked on all
of them and every single one of them at the same
time. Stifling muscle, he made himself small,
suppressed the red of crushing their Adam's apples
with the chapped heel of his hand. He could have
stood wide up and become their worst wall. Instead
he succumbed. He was safe until they began circling,
slow like blaze's first lap at wood, and one of them
zoned in on that sweet spot, that deep blue dip
in his chest that so loud and plainly uttered
Animal.

I also became the mother of the sons and daughters
of my daughters and sons. I am their silvering
nana, plucking sweaty wads of ones from my
bra to pay for rattles and Enfamil and bags
of fluorescent cheese curls because getting drunk
on the orange dust is the only thing that will
calm them. I am the grandmother who becomes
the mother of the flails, squeals and belching
my darling corpses leave behind, I *get up, get
up,* without words replacing what has been
removed. I am a saint quite accidentally, a tired
woman piecing together soldiers who were once

pieced together by the soldiers who were born
to me. My arms are thinned by their pull. I can
only hold on until they find the door I've so
willfully locked, and they burst through. And Lord,
they're armed with what they think are the rules.

July 18, 2011, Denver, CO— Alonzo Ashley, 29, who may
have been suffering from mental illness, refused to stop
splashing his face at a Denver Zoo drinking fountain on a
blistering hot day, then made irrational comments and threw
a trash can. Admitting that he was unarmed, officers killed
him with a taser, citing his "extraordinary strength."

Lord, what are the rules? On the devil's day,
can't a black man stop and scrub off some
season? Can't he talk his core down without
officially explaining? It's not like anyone but
his mama would understand the flow of sweat
beneath his sweat, the outright music his head
told him it's time to and damned alright to sing.

But his corded forearms, the muscle pushing
forward the fix in his eyes, the flared snort
and snot and brick of him. The clenched ass,
the impatient neck, the resplendent neck,
the sweat-crusted neck, the gorgeous neck,
the mad you made him as the heat blew hard
on his tangle, his terrible vast, his towering.
His breath blasting flat and meat like my pot
liquor, his thighs telling the stories of trees.
His thread spiraling too fast aloose. Is what
you saw. Is what you saw. Even though my
boy was light enough to be lifted by a notion,
you punched him with holes so everything
that said *man* aloud would gush out. Murder

helps you sleep at night. Murder
keeps me up at night, thinking of you
asleep at night.

February 3, 2015, Fairfax County, VA— Suffering from
mental illness, Natasha McKenna died after being shocked
four times with a stun gun while her hands were cuffed
and her legs shackled.

I am the mother of the dark magicians,
but sometimes the magic loses its holy
clutch. Natasha should have been able
to slip those shackles long enough to
fire a bullet into the wrong side of her
hair, which would have simplified
the paperwork and left me with a body
unburned to bless. How could she forget
the hoodoo that she knew so well,
breaking loose to be the agent of her
own recapture, hanging herself with
hands that are both free and shackled?
It pains me to think of how she drowned
so utterly in spitted light. If only she
weren't so my accident, I could have
been the hands at her sides. But they
had already chalked her up to fireworks,
and my prayer, the flinging of expletives
into her waning smoke, had nowhere
to go. She wouldn't have recognized my voice.

Once I put this baby in the ground, I'm ready. . . . This means war.
    —Geneva Reed-Veal, mother of Sandra Bland, addressing
        the congregation at Johnson-Phillip All Faiths Church,
        Prairie View, Texas

I don't expect you'll recognize my voice,
no matter that I populate your world
with demons and obstructions, dangerous
assumptions. I'm the mother of the hung,
the misted head, the pistol-whipped, the hands
that found the hands, the tasered crazy girl
and all the magic real that you can stand.
I thought perhaps I'd let you'd see that I
am flesh and bone and pulse, that in the night
I wail with want of them. And yes, I know
I entertain you, digitized, my break
and fall rewound replayed and tabbed. But
now, I fight my own collapse, that ugly twist
that grief brings to my face to make you laugh.
I'm here to say their bodies weren't at war
with you. I'm here to say their bodies weren't
at war with you. I'm here to say their wars
were in their bodies. And the battlefield
was always yours, was always yours, was all.

The Mother Dares Make Love Again, After

I wake with dawn yawning an unbridled itch across the span of
my chest, as if there is a lie that will die if it is not sung. I begin

inarguably alone, raveled in unwashed sheets and cloaked in funk
so slantly rhymed I suspect its drift is what forces my eyes open.

Unnerved by my own lazy arithmetic, I stink this way to stay
lonely, to explain why old fingers won't remember the scarlet art

of turning a man into moan and spectacular dust. I stink to stay
vital, to bless my lumped body with a structure while I wallow

in the want of a flap-mouthed kiss or a dime-store card crammed
with plastic music, mailed by someone who knew me before my

plummet utter and south. Fall into my collapsing circle of arms
because this Tuesday has spiraled wildly and led you here. Fuck

me in the general direction of history. I will teach you to mourn
with your whole damned face, to unreel a keening as crave becomes

remember. The horrid moon splatters glow on these dirty sheets
that still know me as saint, and commands you to weep my life.

IV

SHOOTING INTO
THE MIRROR

Sometimes

Sometimes he shoots into the mirror
and someone, wearing his face, falls.
A mother grieves, but no one hears her
prayer, collapse and caterwauls.

And someone wearing his face falls.
A mama screeches out his name,
then prays, collapses. Caterwauls
are soundtrack as revenge take aim.

His mama screeches out his name,
but payback's on the daddy's mind.
The soundtrack, as revenge take aim,
morphs into dirge. There's not much time,

but payback's on the daddy's mind.
He grabs a gun, he dies. His night
morphs into dirge, there's not much time
to waste. His boys gon' make it right.

They grab their guns. They die. This night
a mama grieves but no one hears her
waste away. *Her boy—he gon' make it, right?*
Sometimes he shoots into the mirror.

Elegy

For my father, Otis Douglas Smith

Splayed, blood-dazzled, lost in an Oriental rug's wry repetition
of roses, you were hours gone. When you were lifted, your light
sifted from shattered seams and the jagged portal in your side
where the bullets nosed for your heat and found it. Your hands,
calloused and shit-hued with nicotine, must have risen to break
the blast. Their tiny bones were everywhere. You etched a mark
on the rug like a riotous running, as if you were hightailing away
even after the thud and crooking groan, one arm straining hard
for a promise north of you. You figured on a bluesman's end—
a scorned, earth-hipped gal screeching *Fool, I told you if I ever,*
your laugh, a thin spry blade easing into you like a sliver of ice
into a dirty jelly glass of JB. But oh, not this. When your time
came, it came with you squared in a fool's shuddering gunline,
you with your incessant Doublemint smack, red-threaded eyes,
rolled wads of ones. Your killer bolted, bragging to the block
that he'd just shot a man and stolen everything he could hold.
Spooked, he tossed the keys to your Lincoln on the car's hood,
caught a bus, couldn't sit for shouting *I just took a man down.*

Like a soldier whose chest begs a star: *Just took a man down,
took him all the way out.* Lowering their eyes, riders shunned
him and his untied sneaks, blotched a browning scarlet. *Hood
rat,* they hissed, ignoring his tale of you, siphoned of last light,
all the way out, your right arm stunned just short of threshold.
As the bus smoked past taverns, sheds of idle worship and side
streets weighted with white men's names, a ragged roadblock
waited to snag your chatty killer. He froze, raised both hands,
the boast of *Took a man down, took a man* fading as his eyes
turned toward his fellow passengers with the old heartbreak

114

of betrayal. And during the swift rolling of credits, that line dividing the two of you wasn't there. You both bore the mark of murder. You were just two of the disappeared, out of time at the exact same time, edges misting, then vanishing the way B-sides go unwailed in the crevices of a jukebox, the way ice gets gone when it's doused with hooch. *Dead* is such a hard lesson across the shoulders. I remember you said not to ever mean goodbye. You said *A story stops breathing when it ends.*

My mama, your wife, loved God so hard that she put an end to Saturday nights, wearing pants, liquor that went down the scarring way. She was a blank for the Lord. She had never dared that part of downtown, where her slow, twisted diction, fraying A-line skirt, Sears cinnamon-tinged hose, and hard-pressed curl labeled her westside, native of the neighborhood no one saw. But that day she rode the Madison bus, in service to her faith and her child, with news that would slap my light shut. *Somebody shot your daddy, he dead,* that was the way she said it, out in a scramble like it truly pained her to hold that graceless weight, like she just couldn't wait for the time to pass the morning from her burden to mine. Planted beside me, wide-eyed, she looked like she'd just made a check mark on her sad to-do list: *1. Tell Patsy 'bout her daddy.* I blocked out the blur of her, her hair sparkling with sweat, the skyline regular as death and death behind us. If she'd held her hand out to me at all, succumbing to some unannounced outbreak of mother, I might have been able to look into her eyes.

Even after my mother, buoyed by churchfolk, glamorized baptism to coax me into a chilly ritual dunking, in the end she had to admit that you were my only god. Unable to break us, she sighed and conceded, wrangled skillets, settled down to her role as bad cop, enforcer, crackerjack of the backhand. My whole childhood, I dodged her justice—*Girl, don't ever sass me, hear?* Grabbing ironing cord, branch, clothesline, she'd crisscross my legs with lashes, snorting an explanation—

Better to get beat in here than kilt out there. I tried to block
the over and over raw engine of her hands, struggling hard
to loose myself, which only made things worse. *Chile, mark
my words, you leavin' here with a lesson.* The neighborhood
pooled beneath our window for the squalling—but the upside
came the next day, after remedies of rubbing alcohol and ice,
when I dared the daylight to show off my welts, taking time
to limp the boulevard, working my wounds 'til the streetlights
came on. Then she'd call me in, reach out like she might hold
me, say instead *You got to mind me. I don't know no other way.*

How did you two stutter into love? I just can't see any way
one of you saw a chance in the other, nothing that justifies
your tie to Annie Pearl, gangly 'bama gal, who broke the hold
the clammy Delta had on her once she hit Chicago—the end
of the line for those hooked by the north star's conjured light.
You, an orphan raised by pitying Arkansas kin, plotted a break
of your own—stuffing your hard valise at dawn, biding time
as the bus poked toward your craving. Two fools from down
south, comin' up after prayin' on it, gluing together a paradise
that just had to be bigger than your hard string of third-hand
days, all filled with white folk sidling up to you with the side-
eye. How long did it take you to know that all you were ever
gonna be was what you already were? Southern childhoods
led to other ways to be born, one-way treks on the pipeline
to the city's swallow. Steered to tenements already marked
with the chalk outlines of your bodies, your fresh addictions
prepped and waiting, you travelers didn't know just how hard
every dawn would become, how hard it would be to block

the old dogged hiss of home in your bones—whole city blocks
kept on pointing south. Chicago's dirty sun hissed that way
too, searing your necks. Up-north alone and lonely, gals hard-
ironed greased hair into sizzling strings, plumped their eyes
with overloads of Maybelline. They forgot their vows to shun
the bad boys—and Daddy, you were scoundrel. Grabbing hold

of saddidy city ways like you'd been born to them, you marked
turf with an Old Spice–scented, dip-hipped stroll from one end
of Warren Street to the other, then down Madison, past lines
of *tsk-tsk-tsking* church ladies and country girls bathed in light
leaking from crooked storefronts. Where in all that womanhood
was my mother? Did she lift those sleepy eyes and cue a break
in your stride, knock you flat with a new language whenever
she giggled behind her hand? Did that smile conjure the time
when she barreled barefoot through the red dust of countryside
to her mama's squeaking screen door? Somewhere on down
the line, you spied her, sugar countrified in Alabama hand-
me-downs, grinning with enough gold to make you notice.

In the Murphy bed, maybe your woman was sallow and ice,
a moan, pretending steel, not knowing whether she should block
your man ways. You'd been in the city so long—your hands
had learned everything. And Annie Pearl needed to find a way
to love you past the new beings you were, so weighed down
in store layaway and stilted grammar, miles from the hard
twang of your backdrop. In the end, you were both blindsided,
still wanting what you thought you'd left behind, your eyes
shocked by the familiar body's lesson. Daddy, not much time
passed before you gave in to ritual, shelving your addiction
to the siren drone of the street. *You take this woman forever?*
and you did, entering a church just that once to vow your hold
on a woman set to be cook and comfort. But each daybreak
changed her in the way of omen. She was vexed by the mark
of tenement, factory and blistering snow. The neighborhood
that opened its arms to her now blocked her breath. In the end,
you heard *honor,* you heard *obey*—locking on to the gilt light
in the eyes of God's best girl, you smiled, signed the dotted line.

Laughing, you told me how she hated being pregnant. Her line:
It'll be a blessing to drop this chile. You fed her chipped ice
to cool her core, warmed stews, tended to her from first light
til last. She ate pigs' feet, salt pork, shaded her eyes to block

the sun wilting the blinds—*It's just too much day.* Pretending
not to be monster, ashamed of her hollering and swollen hands,
she ate, slept deep and snored razors through what motherhood
does. You rehearsed the word *husband* and looked for a way
to tune out your boys, hooting outside, calling out the mark
of bitch in you. Your woman rampaged while working down
a list of everything God said you shoulda been, her heartbreak
wide enough for just the whole world to hear. It was that hard
to be both her sky and root. Everybody knew you couldn't hold
on too long while jukeboxes blared and fine gals strode side
streets, asking, asking—*You seen Otis?* If your wife was ever
blessed to drop that chile, you could dream of laying your eyes
on that rumble 'neath her skirt again—but the assumption
of her rollicking belly meant you were running out of time

to start starting over. And the days were June steam by the time
I came, ripping a way toward air, insisting on your bloodline.
You'd never seen such violence. I clamored, wailed, stunned
you by not being you *or* her, but something other, my raw voice
chronic, not thrilled with the rules of my arrival. Your eyes,
threaded with old spirit, were my first damns given, their light
so wholly tangled with mine. Hours old, I already had our fever.
As soon as I sensed you wanting to flee the birth room, I blocked
out the carping of my mother, drained and bled low on the side-
lines, and focused on winning *you* over. You couldn't even pretend
that the beginning of my story was end of yours—my death-hold
on your finger was a vow. Your wife wailed. I filled your hands.
While she crafted my new, functional name—one we'd find it hard
to live down to—you blankly nodded, succumbing to a parenthood
that was nothing like the one you'd pictured. My lock on you broke
every rule—fast co-conspirators, we were already hatching a way
out of where my birthday found us. My mother was *one down,
none to go* while you and I began a sloppy, blatant love, marked

by my wet gaze and your sweet inability to put me down, marked
by your whisper—*Jimi Savannah, Jimi Savannah*—each time

a new christening, the name you heard when you looked down
at me, slick and gasping in her arms. But Mama went hardline
with the citified *Patricia Ann*—*Jimi's* sassy music became a way
for us to communicate under the radar of her roaring, a fiction
that rooted us in our real. As soon as I was, she vowed to break
our tie so that she could master and suppress us singly—a device
she picked up from the *Do Right By God* manual of parenthood.
She would never stop trying. Even before the moment our eyes
met, Daddy, our woe-be-them script was already written—hard
road ahead, the odds stacked to teeter, our meager guiding lights
flickering dim, born under a bad sign. You wrapped your hands
around my wild squirm and we changed the ending. You'd never
forget the feeling of my new, my barely a day, the feel of holding
the whole promise of north in your grasp. You strutted the block
trumpeting news of baby, but not wife, as if your marriage ended
when I began. Without a history, I was so simple to love. Side-

stepped and mad about it, my mama grew fat and functional. Inside
our tiny three-room, she wiped and scoured, scrubbing every mark
with bleach or Lysol, pressed bedsheets, decided it best to depend
on Jesus for all and everything. She trained an evil eye on the time
whenever you left home, reckoning you were headed for the block
of JB, gutbucket music, red-lipped women who pulled you down
to their open mouths. You ran to spades and brown liquor, holding
on to a thin wad that probably wouldn't last the night. Your timeline
for being right-minded and getting home at a Christian hour never
worked. Instead, you and toddler me devised a plan, a sneaky way
to get you in after curfew once your pissed wife threw up her hands
and chain-locked the only way in. Fighting sleep, I was stationed
in my bed in the front room, drooped eyes trained on the line of light
beneath the door. After a Morse code of coughs and taps at daybreak,
I'd tip to the door, flip open locks, let you in. She came down hard
on us once she woke up to find you inside, popping me once or twice
with the business end of a belt, weeping wide, searching your eyes
for clues to your night. Your answering gaze, measured and hooded,

fueled the flames. I loved our wicked alliance, my falsehoods—
You must have left the latch off, Mama—the hastily plotted inside
job, the you and me always against the her. I loved how her eyes
bulged with our betrayal, her pleas to Jesus gone wide of the mark
while you and I schemed and cheered, proud of our dual sacrifice.
We were definitely an inspired pairing, Patsy and Otis D, the end
and opening curtain of so many dramas. It must have been hard
for her, plopped in front of *Bonanza*'s drone, afraid more time
would only make us stronger. Maybe she considered heartbreak—
but that was a frailty. God say no. It was time for *Lucy*. Blocking
out our whispers, she concentrated on the gray flickering light
of the TV, mesmerized by crisp hilarious white people in downy
garb living the life she was promised. She just wanted a fraction
of it—a real husband home in time for dinner, a husband holding
flowers, toting a briefcase, spewing city words. But *your* hands
stank of smoke and sugar from where you both worked the line,
and her chile was—well, devilish. I know she prayed for a way
past the two of us, Daddy, because I heard her. Kneeling, never

behind a closed door, she wondered aloud if the Lord would *ever*
enter our souls, click the righteous switch, gingerly lift the hood
that cloaked us in sin. While she spent every day in church, away
from our godless chaos, we played race music, mingled outside
with the pimps and double-dutchers. Or we'd get in the long line
snaking into the corner butcher shop. I couldn't take my eyes
off the real pig's head in the window or the flying pink hands
of the butcher. We dragged our feet in bloody sawdust, marked
our nicknames on the shop's wood beams. You loved to hold
up fistfuls of bargain entrails until I squealed, then dig into ice
for bulge-eyed perch so we could stage mock battles, a tradition
distressing those who eyed our soldiers for supper. We'd offend
everyone, defiantly being us, only vaguely fearing the meltdown
she was sure to have when the grapevine buzzed tales of our hard-
headedness. We were *her* kin, edging the Buick through stoplights
with the horn blaring, pairing up like street gangers for fun times

with all the busy anyones and anythings that made our block
hum. Soon she was the stranger in the room. So when the break

finally came, I was left all alone. It was a slow-motion break,
with our Annie Pearl's raw preachy screech as backdrop, never
ceasing: *Y'all are headed for so much hell.* We couldn't block
out all the ways she grew melancholy, faced with the likelihood
she needed God more than we needed her. Our lives were time
passing, faster than she could fix us. She couldn't scream away
our trespasses. When you realized it was finally over, the light
I'd given you streamed from your bodies. I watched. Blindsided
by the end, Annie didn't see that her take on love was a hard
slow kill you put up with just long enough to meet your deadline
as father. You hugged my grieving breath thin, then put me down
whispering *Baby girl, it's not you I'm leaving.* I romanticized
the moment, heard violins swelling over the words THE END
as you and I skipped giddily into a cowboy sunset, our hands
clasped. We would grieve her, of course. Eventual celebrations
would be muted and tasteful. But instead of joining me to mark
the end of your marriage as the real beginning of us, your advice
to me was *Stay here with your mama. I'll be back.* My hold

on you, the clutch that merely defined me, just couldn't hold
on past the wrath of the woman who long ago vowed to break
us away from each other. And toward some God. I paid the price
for your walking away—a gangly ten-year-old who had never
given real weight to the word *alone,* I suddenly decided to mark
my days by disappearing. Words went first. Teachers blocked
out time for meetings with my harried mother once I shunned
speech and slammed silent. Ms. Pearl referred all parenthood
matters to her God the Father, who I'm sure threw up His hands
once my hair began to fall out in clumps and my nighttimes
were spent snot-weeping, praying to my daddy, my god. *Depend
on THIS Father* she'd say, pointing to a plastic crucifix, her way
of making me see you as Him, as both gone and there. Her eyes

were wild all the time. Every morning, when a damnable light
fell upon my face—a face just like yours—she'd break down
and whip me in your name, conjuring sins, turning my backside
to flame. I'd phone you in secret, pouring broken into the line,
begging for you back. Until you decided that no matter how hard

it was to stand tall between her and a deity, no matter how hard
it was to say to her *You can't make me not be her father,* I could hold
you to the wounding pledge *It's not you I'm leaving,* that old line
I wished on while holding my own hair in my hand. You broke
down, came back through our door, and every night you sat beside
me and we traded tales, whispering beneath her wrath. Your voice
was all the yes in the room while a mute Annie Pearl, nailed down
with rage, stayed glued to the Philco and her Lucy Ball. You never
left until I was asleep. You were left alone with her. Then the light
of the boulevard bellowed, and you'd set out to make your mark
on the moon. With a *harrump* and a deadly edition of the side-eye,
my mother would accuse you of seeing other women on our block
(of course you were—how long ago had she picked *her* wary way
around your body's eager landscape?). She gamely auditioned
for a role as the wounded, righteous God-fearing ex, a sly blend
of monster and martyr, and you were undisputed hero of the 'hood,
the romancer, card sharp, devoted daddy. I remember the time
she boldly called you on your rep after I'd been caught red-handed

lifting earrings from Woolworth's: *So YOU spank her.* Your hands
rose and fell with pained hesitation, just twice, your crying hard-
mingling with my pained theatrics. Daddy, how did you make time
for that kind of love? How did you become the someone who holds
on when a southern gal says let go, someone who blesses childhood
with the sharp magic of made-up songs and giddy minutes in line
to gape at the circus of a dead pig's head? So many had to fend
for themselves, alone with bone-lonely mothers. Love let me break
you, daddy, it brought you back, back to me while the loud fiction
of fathers crushed everything around us. Love welled up inside
you like a city, replaced your dreams with what you had, a way

for you write your name aloud. You were my bad daddy, vice
winkling right up front like that gold tooth. You ran every block
with the bittiest rep, five feet of swagger and spice gettin' down
with a sweet hip swerve to anything blue from the juke, your eyes
absolutely glinting with just enough bad juice. Daddy, whatever
possessed you to teach me to drink, vowing no man would mark
me as victim? You spoon-fed me shots of JB 'til my warning light

blasted, dimmed again. I was 16. There you were arched in the light
above me, rapid-firing: *What time is it? Now can you see the hands
on your watch? Tell me what song just played on the jukebox. Mark
or Marvin, what's the bartender's name? OK now, think hard now—
how do you get home from here?* I didn't know a damn thing, never
having been drunk before, but I got better. Now there's not a time
I can't drink a hopeful man under the table with my midnight eyes
wide open. Schooling me in slow dance, you were careful to hold
me at a daddy distance while my whitewashed PF Flyers came down
on your toes again and again. We were the talk of the neighborhood,
crazy Otis knocking at his door like a stranger every day, blocking
out a stream of spiteful screams from his still-wife, making a beeline
to that baby gal so she could have some kinda daddy. Your sacrifice
was born of love that breaks and breaks and rearranges. In the end
it taught me just what a man looks like when he never goes away.
Somebody shot your daddy, he dead were just words alongside
other words, a way for some stranger to finally get my attention.

Your funky apparition sidles up, riding its blue rail, and blasts a light
that makes me laugh out loud. Eerily still at your side, your hands
hold something I can't see. It's daybreak when you make your mark
on my waking dream, a way for us to be together before the hard
business of pretending a life begins. This is something I'd never
practiced, this halfways ghosting, like a sweaty runner making time
with the silliness of a single leg. You're a chalk outline, your eyes
reaching. I quick-slap your hand, unblock the view of what you hold.
Your dead eyes hooded, you lay down the gift. It's *Jimi,* my real name.

The First 23 Minutes of the First Day Without

1. The weather is writ large through the appearance of symptoms:
2. an orange chill, the taxi driver grimacing
3. when he hears your nasty address, muttering
4. *That place is bad* Your mother absent-
5. mindedly rubbing your leg, wondering when
6. you'll get snotty and wobble-eyed   whether you'll
7. hog the limelight by flaunting your ugly blossom
8. of grief   a sin for the daughter to wear the wool
9. of widow
10. Her mantra, *He in heaven now He in heaven now,* synced
11. perfectly to the ruts in the street   The cab blares
12. black cardamom and onion, and the driver's
13. eyes widen as he enters the riotous fringe of
14. *the bad place*   barred
15. Baptist lean-tos   glint
16. snarlers arching toward the windshield   stores
17. selling wax lips and 45s   he
18. stops
19. and there is a sidewalk that still bears the slight
20. weight of your father   there is a row
21. of open mouths   *nonono*   there is a trumpeting sun
22. one whole damn day
23. behind the news

Requiem

It is Tuesday, the wailing church has emptied, and the earth is packed hard over him. She pours a stout tumbler of boundaries and warnings, sips, then opens the heavy volume to page 67: *How to Build An Altar*. She reads the directions aloud.

"Begin with a spine of funked silver—pull it screeching from your body, staple the writhing thing to a board to keep it still. Add a necessary food—Pixy Stix, the inward workings of pig, a fistful of Lemonheads, slippery salt pork collards, a peppermint stick shoved into the core of a thick sour pickle. And damn, don't you be ashamed of chicken—pebbled and spice, sluggish pink blood lovingly preserved in sinkside jars. Sprinkle everything with the stubborn rusted dust from some southern road.

"Decorate the walls of the altar with frescoes of thick-thighed mothers . . ."

She yearns to skip this part, but doesn't.

". . . mothers with hard insisting bellies, double negative mothers, rust-dusted mamas, mamas with no clue, mamas with no husbands or fresh food, mothers with their crowns oiled and pressed hard.

"Add something from the get-pretty room, but not the hot comb—how about the smell of burning and the sizzling suggestion of yourself growing smaller? How about that scar behind your ear, your neck, how about a precious clip from your napped edges?

"Find a place for your hips, a place large enough to hold them as they become engines. String the room with double-dutch clothesline and curled-corner Polaroids of the wounds you still carry because of that rough and roundabout rhythm—abbreviated toes, whip songs on your calves, ankles huge with triple-time and the sidewalk stomp.

"Now ask God what you should do next."

She doesn't ask. She already has a cross, black velvet headshots of Him and him, a hymnal, a funeral home fan. She sips again. She keeps reading.

"Right about now, the devil, all come hither and cosmic slop, will claim his corner. He'll flash his chest muscles and grunt your entire Christian name in a way you ain't never heard before. Ignore him, but keep an eye trained in his direction."

She locks gaze with the chuckling bogey until the page asks: "Chile, did you forget your daddy?"

No. She couldn't.

"Spritz the altar with the Old-Spice-Lucky-Strike-sexed stench of him, the ritual repeating air of factory, the necessary milk of gin and tabasco, the smell of tobacco spittle and an open-mouthed blues groan.

"Did you forget your daddy? Fill a crystal cup with flakes of ash scraped from his forearms, with impossibly thick toenail clippings that drop and make music on hardwood floors. Finish with the sound of the way he said *daughter*—even if he screamed it. Even if he whispered it in his sleep."

She closes the book. It is Tuesday, the church has emptied. She strains to hear his voice. Nothing. The dirt is packed hard over him. Over his open mouth.

And He Stays Dead

You can convince your young body to slide on the cloak of savage—
bare your teeth towards the clock and pretend you don't feel the hollow.

Or you can slap your own face, winding back time, beating yourself
witless until years blur and you convince yourself it isn't real. The hollow

is not menaced by your trilling. It decides to take your body inside it.
You pile on layers of woolens and fiction, trying to appeal to the hollow

as it owns you. Everyone asks *Why is your voice so drained, so moon?*
It's because you are feverishly slipping on mantras that should heal the hollow,

but it just grows larger, and you flail around inside it. It is shaped so
stupidly like a father. You can't find your knees to kneel. The hollow

will be damned if it gives you a chance to pray your way out, so you
will yourself limp and succumb to damage. Passing days seal the hollow.

Daughter, wear your father like a cloak. Flaunt the blue, the gone
stink of him. Those woes are yours, crafted to reveal. You're hollow.

Emmett Till: Choose Your Own Adventure

Turn to page 128 if Emmett Till never set foot in the damned store.

So our Chicago kid runs by the store
instead of being wooed by chewing gum
and peppermints. The steamy shop's a bore
'cause they've got better suckers where he's from.
He's sworn to be remembered in this town,
and so his raucous cousins egg him on
to escapades much sweeter than those found
in candy—live and buzzing skins upon
the water, fruit to yank from every tree.
He hurtles past without a second thought,
without acknowledging her silent plea
behind the screen, her gaze so clearly fraught
with crave. *Hey nigger, welcome to the South—*
come slip my sugar deep into your mouth.

Incendiary Art: The Body

I've nightmared your writhe, glum
fists punching their way out of your
own body, the blind stumble through
the buckled vein of your throat as
your nerve endings sputtered and blew.
I've dipped my finger into a vaporous
pool of your skin. The heat blessed
your whole new self with horizon,
square-jawed boy. With such potent
intent, you blared illicit and just enough
saint. Now, with so many northern
days between us, you are much easier
to God. But they are looking for you.
They are wildly sloshing fuel across
the landscape and they are screeching
your name. Today, one said *I sure would*
like to burn a black man alive. So, yep,
you left us here with undulating acres
of fools and that particular stank leg
of gospel. You left us all this snuff,
hawk and proud little bowleg, you left
their brains stunned by dairy and fat
meat. You left us not much path, even
after your body was that brief beauteous
torch. They seem to remember you
fondly. And there are unstruck matches
everywhere.

Acknowledgments

Grateful acknowledgment is made to the editors of the following anthologies and print and online journals in which these poems first appeared:

Arroyo: "The Then Where"

Asheville Poetry Review: "Reemergence of the Noose"

The Baffler: "Incendiary Art: The Body"

Boston Review: "Shot Himself While Handcuffed" (excerpted from "Sagas of the Accidental Saint")

Buzzfeed: "The Five Stages of Drowning"

Eleven Eleven: "Incendiary Art: Tulsa, 1921"; "Blurred Quotient and Theory"

Epiphany: "Incendiary Art: Birmingham, 1963"; "Requiem"

Golden Shovel: "Black, Poured Directly into the Wound"

Hunger Mountain: "And He Stays Dead"; "Mammy Two-Shoes, Rightful Owner of Tom, Addresses the Lady of the House"

Interim: "When Black Men Drown Their Daughters"

Normal School: "Sagas of the Accidental Saint" (excerpt); "Emmett Till: Choose Your Own Adventure" sonnets; "Incendiary Art: Ferguson, 2014"

Of Poetry and Protest: "No Wound of Exit"

Plume: "10-Year-Old Shot Three Times, but She's Fine"; "BlessBlessed"; "Incendiary Art: Chicago, 1968"; "Incendiary Art: Los Angeles, 1992"; "Incendiary Art: MOVE, Philadelphia, 1985"; "See What Happen When You Don't Be Careful"

Poetry Daily: "Incendiary Art"

Prairie Schooner: "Runaway"

Rattle: "Elegy"; "ReBirthday"

Redivider: "The Mother Dares Make Love Again, After"

Tidal Basin Review: "Hey, who you got in here?"

Vilanelles: "XXXL"

Waterstone Review: "That Chile Emmett in That Casket"; "Enigma of the Shadowbox Swine"

I am eternally grateful to the Guggenheim Foundation for the generous support that permitted me to carve out the time and mental space for this and other projects, and to the MacDowell Colony and Yaddo for providing the invaluable shelter, serenity, and sustenance I needed to create.

Kudos yet again to my patient, persistent, and phenomenal first reader, the indefatigable Kwame Dawes; to my dependable third eye, Roger Bonair-Agard; and to the ultimate editor, my insanely supportive husband, Bruce DeSilva. Thanks to the communities where I teach and learn—the City University of New York, Sierra Nevada College, VONA, Cave Canem, and the Vermont College of Fine Arts—where many of these poems were reimagined, revised, discussed, and debated, and where they first reached air.

Every word is for Bruce, Mikaila, and Damon, who love and are loved relentlessly.

And for every woman who began her morning with a son and ended the day without one.